Good Dads, Bad Dads

GOOD DADS,
BAD DADS.

by

Oluwakemi Ola-Ojo

ISBN 978-1-908015-00-6

Published by
Protokos Publishers
PO Box 48424
London
SE15 2YL
Website:www.protokospublishers.com

Cover Design by Prex Nigeria Limited.
E-mail: prexng_2000@yahoo.com or prexadvert@hotmail.com

Printed in the United Kingdom.

God is to the father what the good
father ought to be to the child.

Jesus Christ is to the Church what the
good husband ought to be to the wife.

The Holy Spirit is to a man what the
good man ought to be to his friend.

ACKNOWLEDGEMENT

God is to be praised for the insight He gave me into the stories shared in this book.

I acknowledge with thanks the support of my mother Mrs. Grace Ojo through whom the idea for this book was inspired as I was talking to her in our home on the evening of January 21, 2002, and throughout my writing this book.

I am grateful to God for my family and friends whose understanding and cooperation continue to bless my life and writing.

Thanks to Mrs. Bisi Omilabu for editing this book.

Thanks to all who found time to read and comment on this book for their invaluable comments and encouragement.

And finally, thanks to Prex Ltd for the unique cover design for this series and to Protokos Publishers for the excellent work they have done in publishing and marketing my books.

CONTENTS

DEDICATION

This book is dedicated to the following:

First, to the Trinity, who in wisdom and love created me and has been my Father at all times, in all places and has unconditionally loved me.

To my godly grandfathers of blessed memory, Chief Timothy Aloba, Chief Gabriel Ojo and late Rev. (Dr.) Emmanuel Akinleye for their fatherly care.

To Chief A. A. Akinbola, Chief J. B. Ojo and Pa (Dr) Olusola Ajolore for being there for me especially when my earthly father could not be there physically.

To Professor Isaacs Sodeye and Professor C. J. Esan, fathers indeed at work whose love and support at critical and crucial times of my life has been very much appreciated.

To all the pastors who fed me with the truth of the living word of God over the years.

To my Dad, Rev (Dr) W. R. Ola-Ojo a 'good father' with outstanding qualities.

To my brothers Jaiye, Oladapo and Olasupo whose acceptability, encouragement, love and support I have graciously benefited from over these years.

To Architect Samuel Adetoro and Engineer Gabriel Ayano - family friends who have been brothers too in several ways at all times.

Thank you all.

INTRODUCTION

This book has been written to examine the lives of twelve fathers in the Bible, their strengths and weaknesses, their opportunities and threats, their successes and failures. It has been written through the eyes of a child, a sister, a wife and a mother who want nothing but success and victory all around for men, especially Christian men worldwide. Its lessons could be applied to kings and peasants, presidents and prime ministers, governors and the governed, pastors, preachers and their congregational members, prisoners and set free men.

Men are ordained by God to lead the families and most women and children would want this to be so too. Every father is like the pilot of the family aeroplane, the captain of the family ship, the driver of the family car.

A man of God once said that any time God wants to bless a people He would choose a father figure through whom He would bless them. Fatherhood is a lifetime responsibility with its challenges, sweetness and bitterness. There is no known school of earthly fatherhood that can be recommended to you as a father but as we examine the lives of twelve fathers in the

Bible together, it is my prayer that the Holy Spirit will enable you as a father to learn from other fathers and that you will be equipped to be a godly father too in Jesus' name. There is no perfect earthly father, so please don't set yourself up for failure, rather examine your life as we study together the lives of these twelve fathers from the Bible and prayerfully ask the Lord to help you where you are failing and for God to strengthen you in your strengths.

You may want to ask me why I have chosen twelve characters to write on. That was the number given to me by the Holy Spirit and those names were the ones given that I should write on. Since then I have become aware of the significance of the number twelve in the Bible. There were twelve sons of Jacob, twelve tribes of Israel, twelve spies, twelve disciples, twelve elders around the throne etc. I have discussed the lives of the fathers in alphabetical order of their names not in the way their story appeared in the Bible. Some of the stories about some of the men discussed cover chapters in the Bible. I have avoided inserting extensive chapters of the Bible in the book and I encourage you to read the Bible alongside the stories in such instances.

This book is one of two in this series. It has an accompanying workbook which could be used for personal study as well as Bible study material for men's groups. Whichever way, the list has not been exhausted.

For those who are not familiar with the Bible who may want to refer to particular incidents discussed, these are highlighted at the beginning of each chapter. May you be a godly father filled with wisdom and abilities to manage and train your children properly in the way and fear of the Lord. May you be a good husband to your wife as Jesus is to the Church and may you be the best friend to your wife and children in Jesus' name (Amen).

WHERE ARE THE GOOD FATHERS TODAY?

Where are the good fathers today?
That is the heart cry of the mothers
That is the desperate plea of the children
That is the great missing link in our society
Where are the good fathers today?

Where are the good fathers today?
Fathers who live in the fear of God
Fathers who lead children by their example
Fathers who are the priests in the home
Where are the good fathers today?

Where are the good fathers today?
Fathers who are not children molesters
Fathers who are not wife abusers
Fathers who do not unleash terror
Where are the good fathers today?

Where are the good fathers today?
Fathers who teach sense and sensibility
Fathers who teach the fear and love of God
Fathers who teach love and respect for life
Where are the good fathers today?

Where are the good fathers today?
Fathers who command respect
Fathers who don't seek to dominate others
Fathers who walk in God's authority
Where are the good fathers today?

Where are the good fathers today?
Fathers who walk in the truth of God's word
Fathers who talk with God's authority
Fathers who speak only the mind of God
Where are the good fathers today?

Where are the good fathers today?
Fathers who teach from their scars
Fathers who will not use birthmarks as an excuse
Fathers who will teach every aspect of life
Where are the good fathers today?

Where are the good fathers today?
Fathers who celebrate each of their children
Fathers who celebrate each child's development
From smiling to sitting, crawling to passing examinations
Where are the good fathers today?

Where are the good fathers today?
Fathers who have one single identity
Transparent in their public and private life
Not minding who is watching, when and where
Fathers who do not bring disgrace to their family.
Where are the good fathers today?

Where are the good fathers today?
Fathers who are genuine protectors of life
Who respect and treasure the miracle of life
Who will take full responsibility for their actions
Not the unborn baby, child or wife abuser or molester.
Where are the good fathers today?

Where are the good fathers today?
Fathers who will treasure, respect and honour
The institution of marriage and godly home
The institution of fatherhood and all that it entails
Fathers who will be God's truthful representative.
Where are the good fathers today I dare to ask you?

© ***O. Ola-Ojo*** *February 2010*

Chapter 1

THE FATHER WHO PROVIDED.

(Genesis 12-25)

Recognising and Obeying God's Voice

The job of a successful father is such that requires hearing from God. He is God's representative to his family. Father Abraham as he was later called heard and recognised the voice of God. There are many voices seeking for our attention daily. To navigate life successfully there is the need to hear, recognise, appreciate and heed the voice of God when He speaks. God speaks all the time if we care enough to listen. He speaks lovingly to communicate His love, guidance, instructions, encouragement, directions and corrections to us when necessary. Amid the voices that are clamouring for our attention do you or can you recognize the voice of the Lord? It is one thing to hear God's voice it is another to recognise that it is God speaking and it is yet another thing to be able to obey Him immediately.

Abraham heard and obeyed God on most occasions. He was the father and the leader of his household, and so are you as a man. Do you know God and can you say that God knows you too? Are you able to hear God in small matters and obey Him? Is your relationship with God such that you can hear Him when He speaks to you anytime and anywhere? Do you trust Him enough to be able to obey Him when He speaks or do you always delay obeying Him? Delayed obedience is disobedience and that could be very costly too. Partial obedience is total disobedience with God. Obedience to God is far better than any of mankind's good intentions.

Many of the times Abraham heard God, he was given specific instructions to follow, which would sometimes involve other people's co-operation. For example, God asked him to leave his country for another land that He would show him. What faith to leave the known and comfortable for the unknown and possibly nomadic life *(Genesis 12:1-3)!* A person's geographical location is important to a person's destiny and often God will ask or reposition someone so as to prosper them. Relocating especially geographically can be challenging, daunting and frightening; leaving the known for the unknown, the familiar for the uncertain territory; and the secured for the exposed. It can be financially implicating, physically demanding, emotionally painful and spiritually isolating for those with strong spiritual relationship with their 'god' or place of worship. Abraham had to believe God and trust God that God was able to keep His promises.

At another time he was to circumcise every male in his household, including himself; this was something unheard of until then *(Genesis 17:23).* This was to be a sign of his covenant relationship with God. Today in some cultures physical circumcision is optional. However, there is still the need for spiritual circumcision, a heart turned from sin and now yielded to God.

There was the time that God asked him to sacrifice his covenant child, Isaac, but God later stopped him from killing that same Isaac as a sacrifice to the Lord his God. Brother what or who is your own Isaac? What will you do if God was to ask for your own 'Isaac'?

Every God-fearing and successful person needs among other things, to hear directly and clearly from God. Can you imagine if Abraham had not heard God when He asked him not to sacrifice Isaac? Oh that the Lord will give each one of us the ability to hear Him so that we can know what to do always. In all of these times Abraham believed God *(and that counted for him as righteousness and he became God's friend).* Abraham's belief in God was seen as he believed that God could:

(a) take him to a better land and bless him.

(b) give him the promised child *(Genesis 21:1-5)* so in his old age he played his role in relationship with his wife.

(c) raise Isaac up after the sacrifice and years later.

(d) send an angel to help his trusted servant get Isaac the right wife.

Build an altar of worship

Everywhere he went, Abraham built altars of worship to God. How central to your life is fellowship with God? Where, brother, is your altar of praise, sacrifice, petition and thanksgiving? While it is good that we are able to worship God everywhere it is also good that we have a visible defined altar or place of worship for your God. It helps your family and yourself to have a point of reference as you praise and pray to God. When do you visit your altar? Is it only when there is an impending danger or fall, success, sickness or problems?

Abraham was certainly a man who was able to carry his wife, son, servants and other people along in following God's instructions most times. Abraham's faith in God was such that when Isaac enquired about the lamb for the sacrifice, he simply replied, *"The Lord will provide" (Genesis 22:5-8).* Your wife and children's faith will be further enhanced when you also allow them to be part of your experiences in God.

Be a positive influence

Abraham was a positive influence on his family and household. He was also a positive influence on Lot, his nephew and Eliezer, his head servant, who went to seek for a wife for Isaac *(see Genesis 24:12-13, 26–27).* What sort of influence are you to your family and household?

Abraham was a man of peace and he avoided family quarrels with his nephew Lot and Lot's servant. Abraham proposed a way out of the quarrels which arose due to shortage of grazing land for their cattle and also allowed the younger nephew, Lot was to choose his own portion of land first. He never complained, murmured or grumbled after Lot left him, so should you never too. As long as it depends on you brother, live at peace with everyone including members of your family. Nothing is gained in family quarrels.

Lot's choice of land left Abraham with the desolate land, yet he did not complain. He must have trusted God. God possibly noted that his nephew had cheated him. God came to Abraham and instructed him first to take a look at the remaining land in the four directions and walk the length and breadth of the land as God was going to give it to him. Abraham obeyed *(Genesis 13:1-18).* Brother, which relative, friend, colleague, house or flat mate have you helped but instead have cheated you like Lot or duped you? Painful as it may be for you humanly speaking, give it to God and see how He will make it much better for you in life. How far can you see in your calling? What length and breadth are you prepared to prayerfully walk and work in order to become all that God wants you to be?

Abraham did not hold any grudge against Lot or abandon him when he later ran into trouble. Rather, he went to rescue Lot and his goods from his captors without enriching himself from the spoils *(see Genesis 14:1-24).* Many of the people you have helped (or those who had taken advantage of you in the past) may later need your help. When that time comes, will you act like Abraham or do otherwise?

Abraham did not enrich himself from other's misfortune when he went to rescue Lot and the others. He could but he refused, convinced that it is only the Lord's blessings that make rich and adds no sorrow to it *(Proverbs 10:22)*.

Abraham was so hospitable to the point that he entertained angels without knowing. He came in contact with some visiting strangers and ministered to them, only to later realise that these strangers were angels. Could this be also testified concerning you too, who is a seed of Abraham by covenant? Do you take advantage of people in need? Can you honestly stand before God and man that your motives for helping any of the less privileged are as pure as you are claiming?

You may be able to justify your actions, but God looks at your motives *(see Proverbs 16:12)*. God's X-Ray can see through anything and anyone at all times and everywhere. The Bible tells us that darkness and light are the same to God *(see Psalm 139:12)*. Mankind cannot outsmart God's CCTV which had been in constant operation before man's existence on planet earth.

Owe no one nothing

Abraham recognised Melchizedek, Priest of the Most High

and offered Him a tenth of all he recovered after rescuing Lot *(Genesis 14:20).* So my question to you is what have you been doing with your tithes? Are you aware that your tithes belong to God and that it should take priority over your other commitments as a proof of your willing obedience to His word? *(Malachi 3:8–9).*

If you live in the United Kingdom, for example, your tithes could be likened to your gross income tax which is deducted from your income before your salary is given to you. The employer takes it on behalf of the government and the government uses it for providing various basic and necessary services. The government never says thank you when it is deducted because they expect every law-abiding citizen and resident to pay tax. Though tithes are not the same as taxes, they have equally significant importance in meeting the basic needs and up-keep of the Church's various ministries. Unlike your income tax, which the Government takes before handing you your pay packet, God allows us to freely bring in our tithes and offerings. God does not force us as He already has enough resources to cater for the world's economic requests and needs. In addition to paying the tithes, true believers must not forget to give their regular freewill offerings. The fact that we pay tithes should not stop us from giving our offerings. In fact, God told Israel not to appear before Him empty-handed. As we give to God, we ought to give to other people. We also need to recognise the prophet, pastor or priest that God has assigned to us in life and give such people gifts within our means.

A popular hymn writer once wrote: *"Count your many blessings, name them one by one and it will surprise you what the Lord has done."* We cannot pay for the 'tiniest' of God's blessings in our lives but we can, at least, honour and thank Him with our offerings. Whilst the tithe is ten percent of our gross income, offering is left to the giver's freewill and in accordance to what he or she can afford. Though God asked for ten percent of your gross income and gifts as tithes, it is not unusual for people to give much more than the ten percent as tithes.

Our attitude in giving matters much more to God than the size of our giving. Remember Jesus watched those who gave into the treasury and only commended the widow who gave two pennies *(see Mark 12:41-44).* We should give our offerings with expectation of returns, not just only of money, but also of healing, breakthrough, deliverance, protection, etc. We ought to name our seed when we give, and give as God leads us; sowing into fertile grounds. Though our tithes are to be paid to our local churches, we should, however, always endeavour to give offerings and gifts to other ministries as the Spirit of God leads us. Business owners should also pay tithes on their business income and give offerings. I have seen many businesses grow and expand rapidly when they do so. Churches and ministries are also encouraged to sow into other churches and ministries as they are led of God.

Change your name

Abram had his name changed by God from Abram to Abraham *(father of many nations).* His former name, Abram, talked about his past while his new name Abraham, talked about his secured future in God. After his name change, nothing seemed to be happening for a while he was still childless, yet he kept answering this new name and, at God's appointed time, he entered into his destiny with the birth of Isaac.

Friend, I want to admonish you to hang in there like Abraham did, and the same God can change your name from childless, drug addict, wife abuser, child molester, thief, liar, etc., He will in His time come through for you too! Amen!

Food for thought: Abraham was called the father of faith; what name are you (or will you be) called? He trusted in Jehovah God; in whom do you trust?

It is important to note that Abram had times when he struggled with his imperfections. For instance, when there was famine in the land he decided to relocate to Egypt. We are not told that he consulted with God before he took this step. Fear must have taken a hold of him as he implored Sarai, his wife, to protect him by lying that she was his sister *(even though this was partially true).*

Thanks be to God who in His mercies prevented Sarai from being molested by Pharaoh *(see Genesis 12:10-20).* It is sad to see some husbands today exposing their wives to situations such that they are willing to let them have affairs with their bosses or a more wealthy man or become a prostitute or even be killed in order to gain promotion or wealth! My brother, your wife is to be cherished and loved only by you as long as you are alive—she is not to be passed around or used as a means to an end. So ask yourself, in what ways have you lied and asked your wife to cover up for you? In what ways have you or are you exposing your wife to the 'wolf' of this life?

It is possible that Hagar was one of the maidservants given to or bought by Abram and Sarai while they sojourned in Egypt. This gift later turned out to be a serious source of grief for them. When you go where God has not ordained for you, you might end up with what starts off like a good bargain, purchase or gift bringing problems you never bargained for later.

God promised to make a great nation of Abram *(see Genesis 12:1-3).* His descendants were to be as many as the dust of the earth *(see Genesis 13:14-16),* and as many as the stars of heaven *(see Genesis 15:1-6).* There was never a time God told Abram that his descendants would be through any other woman apart from Sarai his wife. Abram unfortunately listened to the voice of his wife and had a son through Hagar, their Egyptian maid.

It is one thing for a father to be in tune with God, but it is another thing for him to be obedient to the voice of God, no matter the situation. God's covenant was between Himself and Abram. In listening to Sarah, a third party he disobeyed God. From my experience, years ago God told me that His divine revelation needs no second opinion.

The son that Abraham had through Hagar did not bring lasting peace or joy to either him or Sarah. Invariably, he had to send Hagar and Ishmael away. God's promises can never be fulfilled through fleshly efforts. Even the provision Abraham made for Hagar and her son was so inadequate for their trip that it took the divine intervention of God to spare Ishmael from dying of thirst in the wilderness *(Genesis 21:15–20)*. As a father, if you have in any way made mistakes like Abraham by having children from some other woman *(or women)* other than your wife, you should please make adequate provision for their upbringing especially in the fear of the Lord.

Be an intercessor and trainer

Abraham was a good intercessor. First, he interceded for the life of Ishmael *(Genesis 17:17–21)*. He later interceded for Sodom and Gomorrah because God shared His plan of destroying these lands with him *(Genesis 18:17-33)*. How intimate is your walk with God? Is it such that He can share certain secrets with you? God is still sharing His secrets today in dreams, word of knowledge, word of wisdom and in vision.

Sometimes the Holy Spirit may drop the name of a known or unknown person or situation into your spirit. We like Abraham should immediately pray and intercede until we get a release in our spirit at such a time. You may have to telephone, write, send an e-mail or text message or visit that person if it is practicable. God will share His secret trusting that you and I will act on the information we receive and immediately too. God shared His secret with Abraham saying in *Genesis 18:19* –'for I know that he will command his children and his household after him, and they shall keep the way of the Lord, to do justice and judgment: that the Lord may bring upon Abraham that which he hath spoken of him' Father, can God trust you that you will train or teach and command your children to fear Him in this godless society today? How much of the fear of God do you have in your heart as a father? For you can only give what you have not what you don't.

Abraham and Sarah also had to struggle with infertility even though their livestock were very productive and they had numerous servants from among whom he was able to raise an army of more than three hundred men to rescue his nephew, Lot *(see Genesis 14:17).* It is interesting to note that Abraham did not prevent his servants from having children despite his own obvious barrenness. What are you singly or jointly with your wife struggling with? The answer is in Jesus Christ not in human alternative.

Abraham's training of his household yielded dividend in the day of battle. Maybe you and your wife are facing the same challenges of barrenness, I implore you to please take your pains to the Lord in prayer because God is able to handle your pains and your cries for help.

Prepare to be tested

When Isaac eventually came, God tested Abraham by asking for this long awaited promise as a sacrifice *(see Genesis 22:1-4).* Abraham obeyed God without any reservations or delay by proceeding on a three-day journey to Mount Moriah with Isaac and two of his servants early the next morning.

The three days trip was enough time for Abraham to change his mind yet he did not. The Bible tells us: *"Then on the third day Abraham lifted up his eyes, and saw the place afar off. And Abraham said unto his young men, Abide ye here with the ass; and I and the lad will go yonder and worship, and come again to you" (verse 5).* You need to get to the place where God told you. There are times when you may have to ask some people to wait behind so they don't damage your dream, dampen your faith or hinder you from fulfilling God's plan for your life.

Abraham had prepared the altar and was ready to sacrifice Isaac when God suddenly showed up with an alternative that He had provided. In the face of difficulty, Abraham's confession was of faith in Jehovah God and not in the situation *'the Lord will provide a sacrifice for Himself' Genesis 22: 6-8.* His confession was in the one greater than himself, pointing Isaac to Jehovah God. In the face of problems, who do you point to and who is your source of reference? He also expressed this faith to his accompanying servants telling them that he and Isaac would return to them after the sacrifice *(Genesis 22: 5).* God blessed Abraham and he had many cattle. He dug wells and named them. Years after Abraham's death, Isaac dug the wells again and gave them the same names. There is life and wealth in the well. No wonder Isaac said 'the Lord has made room for us therefore we shall now prosper' and he sure did *(Genesis 26:24).* Brother, what family business or investment are you doing? Or which well have you dug or are digging that your children can continue now and later? Are you exposing your children to your business and how to run it properly and profitably?

Be a provider

Abraham made sure that his son Isaac, the carrier of God's promises was properly married and he made the adequate provisions for that. As he commissioned a trusted servant to this seemingly difficult assignment, his confession was in his trust in Jehovah God not in anything or anyone else *(Genesis 24:6–7).* While it could be argued that many of today's youth would not want a pre-arranged marriage as they prefer choosing for themselves that does not preclude you as a father from getting involved in counselling and prayers for this with your children and as early as possible in their life. A good father will make provisions for the marriage. For those whom the Lord has called into marriage, it is of great importance to be married to the right person as your destiny could be enhanced or aborted by whom you marry.

Even in his sorrow, Abraham did not take advantage of the people of Hebron, but paid in full the price for a family burial place. He thought generationally and planned for a decent place of burial for his family. He gave Sarah a decent burial.

Abraham made sure he had a will in place that settled his wealth between his children *(Genesis 25:1-6).* As a father and brother do you have a written will in place for your family should God decide to call you home now? A will unwritten exposes your family and loved ones to many heartaches and loss of wealth to the government in the UK for instance. A godly father leaves an inheritance for his children's children not debt as the men in the stories of *2 Kings 4:1-8 & 1 Kings 17:10-12.* In this day and age, life/health insurance does not indicate a lack of faith in God but wisdom and adequate provision for yourself and family. Should you be no more, what provisions do you have in place for your family? For those who own their business or company, insuring it against fire, theft and other peculiar risks is wise too. What provision have you made for all the stages of your children's life including their education or vocation?

Perhaps you would like to say a prayer for yourself now as you compare your life with Abraham's life and get it right with

God from now on. You may wish to say a prayer like this:

Father in heaven,
I thank You for the life of Abraham which I have just studied. I thank You Lord for the following areas where I am struggling and need Your help (you might want to list these areas here). Lord I come just as I am asking for Your help, strength and grace. Father, You know how I have been cheated and duped by (list or mention it) Please give me a multiple replacement for all my loss in Jesus name. I want to know You Lord and be Your friend, please make me a fruitful and faithful father too. Bless all those whom I have responsibility for and make me a positive influence over their lives in Jesus' name I pray with thanksgiving. Amen.

Chapter 2

THE FATHER WHO DID NOT REPRIMAND HIS CHILDREN.

He was the last boy in the family with seven brothers before him. His mother's name was never mentioned in the Bible nor did he refer to her.

Who was he?

The Bible introduces David as a shepherd boy alone on the fields. Why was David the last born asked by their father Jesse to tend the sheep alone and not the older ones or with any of his brothers? We do not know perhaps it was the norm at that time or perhaps it was because David might have been a result of a one-night stand affair or born out of wedlock *(Psalms 51:5)* and as such keeping him away from home could reduce the shame and stress on his father. As a shepherd boy he was exposed to many attacks from wild animals and on many occasions stared death in the face as he tended his father's sheep. He looked up to God for his protection and did not complain to Jesse. He was not afraid to be alone in the fields.

In the fields by himself he learnt so much about all of God's creation as recorded in the Psalms he wrote, he perfected his skill on the harp (musical instrument) and the slings with stones. He learnt to defend his life and that of the helpless sheep from the lions, bear, cobra etc. early in life all alone by himself in the wilderness. David was bold and strong enough to kill a lion and a bear single-handedly. David knew God and had a personal relationship with God from when he was in the backside of the wilderness. David was a good shepherd, bold and strong to kill the lion and the bear single-handedly saving the sheep from bears and lions. David was caring and protective of the sheep in his care. Sheep are helpless animals that depend so much on the shepherd. Little did David realise that while he was looking after the sheep, God was training, testing and equipping him in His school for the day when God would appoint him over the whole nation of Israel. May I just say that in God's training school for His children, each one of His children have a personally designed programme where promotion is not automatic nor based on age or status; many times requiring God's training and testing before one could be promoted to the next class of greater responsibility and calling.

Do not underestimate your children!

Brother, what are you doing now? Don't despise it for who knows what God is preparing for you to do in the future. Please do whatever your hands find to do well and without complaining. By the time David fought and killed the lion and bear, no one was there to applaud him, the sheep could not clap for him or tell the world, but God saw it all and was accurately taking notice of him. Brother, be sure God sees you at all times, in all situations and much more He knows who you are and sees through your mind and He is accurately taking notice of you. Remember Joseph, Portiphar's administrator and jailer's administrator who ended up being Egypt's first Prime Minister?

Brother, your birth or childhood circumstances need not hold you bound any longer. Turn it over to God who created you, loved you and has a future for you *(Jeremiah 29:11).* Pour out your heart to Father God, He can handle it and in His presence there is no need to fear or be ashamed for anything including your feelings. It is all right to cry if that will make you feel better rather than bottle up your emotions. 'But ye are a chosen generation, a royal priesthood, a holy nation, a peculiar people; that ye should shew forth the praises of him who hath called you out of darkness into his marvellous light: Which in time past were not a people, but are now the people of God: which had not obtained mercy, but now have obtained mercy' *(1 Peter 2:9-10).*

At a very young age David tended his father's sheep in the wilderness alone. His father when asked to present his sons before Samuel the prophet did not include David. Why? perhaps Jesse felt it was going to be too much trouble to include him in the line for consideration to become a king or perhaps indeed David was a love child or perhaps due to the distance and time it would take to get David back home so Jesse didn't want to present him to the prophet therefore he did not send for him from the wilderness. It can be very painful to be underestimated by any one especially your family members or friends. It would seem to one that Jesse either did not know his son enough as to identify his gifting or he was unaware of David's credentials as he alone watched over his flock. *(1 Samuel 16:5-11).*

David was underestimated first by his earthly father who did not think he was a likely person to be anointed as king. Thanks be to our God who sees the intent of man's heart and whose choice is best. David the little shepherd boy, most despised in the family, was anointed in the very presence of his family by Samuel the prophet *(1 Samuel 16:1-13).* The earthly father's probably rejected son became the Heavenly Father accepted son. In fact, no one was allowed to sit to eat at the feast until David came from the fields. Brother, the fact that due to many circumstances of life has made your earthly parents to reject you does not mean God will not accept you just as you are right now. To God your creator, you were in His mind before the foundation of the earth came into being.

David narrowly missed not being chosen or anointed as a king for Samuel nearly chose the wrong persons instead of him. Brother, there is need for prayers that your own heavenly God designed package of blessing, honour and promotion will not be given to another no matter what. Prayerfully consider this song:

PASS ME NOT

Pass me not, O gentle Saviour,
Hear my humble cry;
While on others Thou art calling,
Do not pass me by.

Refrain
Saviour, Saviour,
Hear my humble cry;
While on others Thou art calling,
Do not pass me by.

Let me at Thy throne of mercy
Find a sweet relief,
Kneeling there in deep contrition;
Help my unbelief.
Refrain

Trusting only in Thy merit,
Would I seek Thy face;
Heal my wounded, broken spirit,
Save me by Thy grace.
Refrain

Thou the Spring of all my comfort,
More than life to me,
Whom have I on earth beside Thee?
Whom in Heav'n but Thee?
Refrain

www. http://www.cyberhymnal.org/htm/p/a/passment.htm
Words: Fanny Crosby, 1868; first appeared in Songs of Devotion by Howard Doane (New York: 1870).
Music: W. Howard Doane, 1870 (MIDI, score).

Dad, how well do you know your son or children? What are their likes, dislikes, strengths, weaknesses, areas of their struggling, phobias, aspirations and desires? How much time do you spend with each child on a daily or weekly basis and what do you or do not get to do with your child or children in this spare time? If you cannot encourage that child then please do not discourage them in any way, as words could be heavier and more destructive than stones.

Know yourself also

David was probably not liked from childhood by his own blood brothers and was underestimated by his big brother *(1 Samuel 17:13-29)*, he was underestimated by King Saul *(1 Samuel 17:31-33)* However this time around David told King Saul his own curriculum vitae (CV) making mention of his transferable skills and wisdom with dealing with animals in the wild thus declaring himself qualified to fight and overcome Goliath the giant *(1 Samuel 17:34-37).* He refused bluntly to be underestimated. Dad and brother, rise up and write your own CV and trust the Lord to make you the most suitable candidate for the job you are applying for or the task that the Lord has committed into your hands.

The world is a battleground with real Goliaths such as poverty, sickness, injustice, unemployment, threats and attacks, etc. While Saul and his army saw the physical size of Goliath and referred to him as a giant, David saw him as an uncircumcised easy prey to destroy for him through Jehovah. How you see your Goliath will determine your reaction and action, launching a physical response to your Goliath or using your man made weapons will fail. It is in the name of the Lord that victory be guaranteed.

Make a good first impression

Equally important brother, you should learn to dress for where you are going or aiming to be because of what I call *'the agent of the 1st impression' as* you are often seen before you are heard. It has been in existence since the Bible times. *See 1 Samuel 17: 17 and 33.* When Saul saw David on the battlefield, not only did David look so young, he was also dressed as a shepherd not as a soldier or warrior, so the natural tendency was for Saul to look down on him. It took David some time and effort to convince King Saul that he was capable of killing Goliath.

When Saul was finally convinced, he felt David's dressing did not match the occasion and so offered him his own military wear. Please do not be careless with your dressing.

Disguised opportunities discovered through obedience

David was exposed to many dangers as a lad yet he was obedient to his father when he was asked to look after the family sheep single-handedly; when he was sent for in *1 Samuel 16:11-12;* when he was asked to take food to his brothers and their Commander at the war; when he was asked to go to King Saul and serve him in *1 Samuel 16:14–23* etc.

Unknown to David, his destiny was locked up in his obedience to his earthly father. Can you imagine what could have happened when his father sent for him as instructed by Samuel the prophet or if he had refused to take some food to his brothers at the war front with the Philistines? What opportunities he would have missed. It is not uncommon that our destiny is locked up in obedience to God primarily and in obedience to those who have authority over us. Brother, how obedient are you, under whose authority are you and how obedient are you to that authority?

Know your tools

David was familiar with his weapon of war which he used as and when required. Dad, what is your weapon of war? And are you familiar with using it or in the face of the battle do you seek for another man's weapon? Please do not underestimate what is in your hand; do not be tempted to think that what you have is inferior to what another person has. Life will many times want to put you down or discount what you have or your gifting but remember that thing in your hand, that skill if prayerfully and carefully channelled is all you need for the battle *(1 Samuel 17:38-43).* If you will turn over to God what is in your hand, God will bless, use and multiply it to achieve His purpose through you. Moses' rod was turned into the rod of miracles, the widow's jar of oil was turned into barrels of oil, David's sling and stones were turned into weapons of great destruction, Paul's pen was used to write about half of the New Testament. What do you have and what is in your hand?

Saul and his army saw the height, size and weapons of Goliath and were afraid but David saw Goliath as an uncircumcised Philistine who was defiling the name of Jehovah. How you view your changes or challengers will determine your reaction and subsequent action.

David was challenged to fight Goliath because he wanted to take away the reproach from Israel, defend the name of the Lord and remove the defilement against the living Lord and His army. Father, how concerned are you for the name of the

Living Lord and His people? How far are you willing to defend the name of your maker or do you tend to compromise so that you are seen as not different from the crowd? Levi's anger was cursed by Jacob in *Genesis 49:5-7* however the curse was broken and turned into blessings when his seeds defended the name of the Lord *(Exodus 32:26-28, Deuteronomy 33:1, 8-11).*

Brother, how do you react to the injustice, oppression, poverty, sickness, lack, etc. around you today? Do you wish you could help or it really does not matter as long as your own children or family members, your country or community is not involved? What do you have that if surrendered to God could bring a permanent solution to the problem you identified? If not yourself, your time, your money or skills could be useful at such a time as this. All that was on David were the sling and the stones, yet when he committed them to the Lord they were sufficient for the necessary victory over the enemy.

As it was that Goliath was harassing the Israelites, so it is that there are Goliaths such as poverty, disease, barrenness, undue delays, untimely deaths, and so on harassing individuals, families and clans defiling the name of the Lord whom we claim to serve. Brother, as a child of God you are in the Lord's army and it is time you depended on God and on His name, face the Goliaths that have defiled the name of the Lord in your family and clan.

Before David fought with Goliath, he checked it out that his efforts would be rewarded by the king *(1 Samuel 17:25-30)*. Father and Dad, it is not wrong to expect to be rewarded for your well-intentioned efforts. Please check that deal, job, or business out before proceeding any further *(Proverbs 22:29)*. David's victory over Goliath guaranteed his father's freedom from taxes. What a huge financial relief that must have been in those days. That same victory brought his family especially his father into the lime light of the community. Each of your acts will bring blessing or otherwise to your family and loved ones. You can terminate every evil counsel in your family by your singular victory over the family Goliath.

David was so sure of his God's support in the battle against giant Goliath. How much do you know God and how sure are you of Him rescuing you in the time of war? Remember the Lord is the 'man of war' and it is He who decides the winner before the fight. David was strong and brave. He trusted God to protect him from the giant and was brave in his words and approach to Goliath.

Many get blessed directly from their primary vocation but many others get blessed or are moved from the prison to the palace suddenly as a result of them using their hobbies to help others. When it was time for Joseph to become what God had planned for him, the Lord remembered him and He caused his gifting of interpretation to be the instrument of his promotion *(Genesis 41:14–46)*. Don't despise your hobbies or gifting. Ask God daily to remember you and lead you into your destiny.

David as a boy alone on his own knew how to please God. He was the only referred to in the Bible as a man after God's own heart. In the wilderness of life, David learnt to personally relate to and with God: as he sought the face of the Lord, he learnt to worship God and he received fresh revelations from God as recorded in the Bible. He was not bitter but learnt to look up to God as a father pouring out his heart and cries to Him. Unlike his predecessor Saul, he learnt to seek the face of the Lord first in his decisions *(1 Samuel 30:1-8).* He like any other man failed woefully, committing adultery and murder but when confronted by Nathan the Prophet unlike Saul, David confessed his sin and repented of it. He fasted, mourned and interceded for his sick child *(2 Samuel 12:1-13).*

David knew how to please God. He was more of a God pleaser than a man pleaser. He was a worshipper of God; he openly expressed his love for God and was quick to admit his wrong doings to God. David saw God literally in everything around him from the vegetation to the animals, in mankind, on the battle field etc. He was also able to convey the attributes of God simply to us in the Bible, for example, *Psalms 23:1-6*

1 The Lord is my shepherd; I shall not want.
2 He maketh me to lie down in green pastures: he leadeth me beside the still waters.
3 He restoreth my soul: he leadeth me in the paths of righteousness for his name's sake.
4 Yea, though I walk through the valley of the shadow

of death, I will fear no evil: for thou art with me; thy rod and thy staff they comfort me.
5 *Thou preparest a table before me in the presence of mine enemies: thou anointest my head with oil; my cup runneth over.*
6 *Surely goodness and mercy shall follow me all the days of my life: and I will dwell in the house of the Lord for ever.*

Brother, are you able to see God in everything such that with anything and everything you are able to teach your children about God *(Deuteronomy 4:6- 9)*. David was multi-skilled and multi-talented: he was a shepherd, a singer, an instrumentalist, a poet and a brave warrior. He equally utilised all his skills as demand was made of them mostly to the Glory of God and the blessing of God's people. Brother, have you discovered all your God-given gifts, talents, or skills? What are your skills? How well are you using these skills and who is benefiting from your use of the skills?

Focus on God not your battles

David was humble and wasn't too keen on being an in-law to the king although he later did. He did not allow the women's praises to enter his head and he willingly served in King's Saul's palace. David obeyed King Saul in fighting his battles successfully and was very well-behaved in spite of the hostile environment around him. He fought and won many battles for King Saul. Brother, living or working in a harsh or hostile environment should not be a reason for your lack of success or bad attitude. God has put you there for a certain reason; if you and I will focus on Him, He will fight our battles and grant us success.

He respected God's anointing on King Saul and would not harm or kill him when he had the opportunities even though King Saul was trying to kill him. It does not matter how those in authority over us behave, we are not to despise God's anointing on them. The least we can do is to pray for them but we must learn to allow God to meet up with their wickedness, injustice, etc. Unlike his predecessor, David sought the face of the Lord in every situation before acting or reacting. When he was running away from King Saul, he stopped to see the priest and sought for God's counsel. He sought the Lord at other times too.

David was a responsible man who settled his family where he felt they were safe while he was running away from King Saul who had wanted to kill him. He lived in the cave but even there, protected those who came to him for help. A life in the cave was certainly contrary to his anointing to be next King of Israel. He did not complain or murmur but learnt to trust God the more, defend himself and others as well as allow God to develop his character there. It is not unusual that in between God's promise and the fulfilment of His promise, there will be times of trial and tribulation, raging storms and winds, but in it all if we hold our peace and allow God to develop our character, His promises as previously revealed will surely come to pass. Father and brother, how responsible are you in providing for your family when times are hard or when the going is tough?

While David and his men went to help king Achish fight his battle, their settlement was raided and the raiders took away all their properties, wives and children. Before you help another person, brother, how secured is your home, family and business? Why leave your family exposed while you go trying to fix other people's business? The true success that a man could have is first within his home. By the time they returned and learnt of the incident, David and his men wept very bitterly. Then his men for whatever reasons decided to kill him. Though David's men planned to kill him because of their loss, I believe because his ways were pleasing to the Lord, God made his men at that time to be at peace with him and not carry out their initial death plan.

Encourage yourself in the Lord

David then encouraged himself in the Lord. There comes a time in life when you need to be alone with God encouraging yourself in Him like David. When last brother, did you encourage yourself in the Lord and for how long will you be running after one man of God or the other in that situation or for that problem? That is not to say godly counsel should not be sought if and when needed. Times of encouraging oneself in the Lord could be very refreshing and rewarding. David did not run away from his men but he sought the face of the Lord asking Him: if he should go after the raiders; if God would help him to overtake them; and if God would help recover the stolen properties and family members. God speedily answered him and in obedience, he went after the raiders, overtook them and recovered all.

Be a blessing inspite of your tribulations

Even though God assured David that he would recover all, God did not give him the strategy. On his way in search of their captured families and goods, David's men saw a man who was almost dying of hunger and thirst. He could have overlooked the man because of his own problems but he stopped and in ministering to this abandoned, hungry and thirsty man he was given the description of how to locate his lost families and goods. In spite of your pains and losses and what you may be going through, it is always refreshing and rewarding if you could stop and reach out to another probably less privileged one or someone with a more serious situation. No one can tell with whom God has provided the key or solution to a challenge.

Father and brother, what have you lost in life that has been making you cry both inwardly and outwardly? What has the enemy stolen from you or your family that is grieving your heart each time you think about it? What has been lost or stolen that is making your joy not to be full? It could be your wife, job, health, career, marriage, children etc. If it means that much to you, then it is worth seeking the face of the Lord and recovering all from the enemies camp first on your knees in prayers then using the strategy that the Lord Himself will reveal to you.

Discipline, integrity and self-worth

David was from a poor family background but with God's favour, Jonathan the heir to Saul's throne became his friend. David did not exhibit any form of inferiority or superiority complex in the friendship. He did not abuse the trust nor enrich himself unnecessarily through the friendship. David was a good and loyal friend especially to Jonathan, Saul's son and heir to the throne. He was not jealous of his friend and he loved Jonathan unto death. He mourned sincerely for the death of King Saul and Prince Jonathan and saw to it that they were properly buried.

David was a covenant maker and covenant keeper. He was a restorer to Mephibosheth and he elevated him to sit at the king's table with him to eat not minding his physically deformity *(2 Samuel 9: 1-8)*. Are you a promise keeper? Can you be trusted to keep a promise to a now deceased person especially looking after the person's family or assets? Have you taken the advantage of the person's disability, death or distance to rob them or deny them of their benefits, assets, inheritance and sweat? The blood of Jesus cleanses us from all sins and elevates us to sit and enjoy all of God's richest blessings as laid out on His table.

It is a known fact that one sin usually tends to lead to another sin and then another sin and on and on; the list is inexhaustible. As a father, being in the wrong place could be catastrophic if care is not taken. Doing the wrong thing always bears a price tag that the father and sometimes his generations will have to pay for very dearly. If you as the father are in the wrong place at the wrong time even now, you might be exposing yourself to some unnecessary evil; seeing the wrong things or having affairs (including business affairs) with the wrong people. Have you as a father covenanted your seeds into the occult or mafia? Cheer up for there is hope for your redemption and your seed's in Jesus Christ.

Life is a battlefield, where are you, father, at the time of war? A war that could be over your family's health, wealth, well being, success, protection, or heavenly provision for your family. Don't wait for a disaster before you take your position at the battlefield. Now is the time father that you need to take up your position and be at alert.

Being a father is much more than procreation or giving a child or your children life and material wealth, children want to be trained by godly fathers who provide them with information, teach them not only by words but more so by example. Fathers who can spend quality time with them and love them unconditionally. Fathers who will correct in love and applaud every single achievement whether it is of the child crawling or taking his/her first steps or passing an examination.

David took Uriah's wife unlawfully and committed adultery with her *(2 Samuel 11–12:23).* He then sent her back home thinking he had got away with that. May I say, sin is like smoke, difficult if not impossible to cover up. When he was told about the resulting pregnancy from the adulterous incident, he attempted to cover it up by inviting Uriah home from the battlefield. Unlike David, disciplined Uriah did not fall into temptation and in the end to cover up his sin, David murdered Uriah by his instructions to Joab. In my experience most of the women wanting a social abortion do it because of the man involved who wants his identity protected or does not want to take the responsibility for the pregnancy. In trying to protect your identity brother whom have you killed or are you killing, how many babies and perhaps their mothers have you sentenced to an untimely death? If the blood of Abel cried from the soil to God for vengeance imagine what will happen should the blood of these innocent ones petition for vengeance?

David took Uriah's wife out of lust. Dad, how have you wrongly used your authority and taken what does not belong to you? It may be some money, other people's wife or property? Yes, as the boss you feel your sin has been concealed from the human eye but remember the song that says, "For our Father who's above, is looking down on earth, oh be careful little hands, feet, etc. what you do." To whom much is given much is expected. Dad, be aware, God sees it all, that which you had thought has been carefully concealed He has seen and you cannot deceive Him *(Proverbs 5:21).* David repented in remorse and fasted of his sins when confronted by Prophet Nathan. God pronounced His judgement on David for his affairs with Uriah's wife and Uriah's death. David's sin then opened his family to many problems from then on. Because of some fathers or fore-fathers, some children are suffering untold calamity or hardship till today. Much as God chose David yet He did not spare his sin. To whom much is given more if not much more is expected.

If you are guilty as David then please pause and say this prayer:

> *Father, I come to You to confess my shameful and heartless deeds. I have wrongfully taken the following things that belong to others (please name as many as you can remember). I have lusted and forcefully slept with other men's wives. I have not taken the responsibility of the resulting pregnancies and or have tried to cover my tracks by killing and/or aborting innocent lives. I now realise how terribly sinful my lust and adultery have caused others. Lord, I come confessing to You against whom I have primarily committed this wrong and I ask Lord for an inside out forgiveness and cleansing by the blood of Jesus Christ and through His name I pray with thanksgiving. (Amen).*

'The worst eye opener is sin

The worst sin is that of disobedience
The greatest disobedience is disobeying God's law or principle'.

Reaping what you sow

In involving Joab in his dirty work to murder Uriah, David made himself become vulnerable to Joab because of this secret. Dad, who have you now become vulnerable to? Which ungodly relationship have you had to keep servicing because of a secret that they kept for you?

Afflicted because of the father's sin

The first child that came from David and Bathsheba became ill due to God's visitation on David's sin. That particular child was struck with a disease and death due to his father's sin *(2 Samuel 12:1-19)*. Father, in what ways have you made your child or children undergo any form of torture or disease due to your sin? Many children today suffer and die of so many diseases, HIV inclusive as a result of being conceived through an infected father or mother. The price of sin cannot be calculated so please spare your wife and children from untold suffering or hardships or untimely death or any combination of these by living right always.

Personal flaws and costly mistakes

David failed to discipline his son Amnon who had raped his half-sister Tamar. Failing to act as a father on this occasion gave room for Absalom to sort the matter out. The consequence of which was that there were more murders in David's family afterwards *(2 Samuel 13).* When you fail to act as the father and head of the family, someone else will step in and do not blame them for whatever wrong decision is then taken.

David failed to discipline Absalom for murdering his half-brother Amnon, for burning down Joab's field and for trying to dethrone him. The consequences of which were the untimely death of Amnon, his having to flee for his life from Absalom, his wives were publicly defiled by Absalom on the roof top *(2 Samuel 16:21–22),* an unnecessary war and the untimely death of Absalom too *(2 Samuel 18).*

David slept with women but it did not seem he loved any of those women. Do you love your wife or you married her and have stayed married to her to use or and possibly abuse her to siphon her health, energy, wealth, influence or affluence? Rejoice in the wife of your youth and let her breast alone comfort you – *(Proverbs 5:18-19).*

David had problems with women, he had many wives, and his lack of discipline in this area became iniquity with his children. Absalom publicly slept with his father's wives on the roof top, Amnon raped his half-sister, Solomon even with his unequalled wisdom had three hundred wives and seven hundred concubines and in his old age, the women turned his heart against the Lord.

Father, whatever flaws are in your life or family unless you deal with them on your knees in prayer to God and have a breakthrough, these same flaws will surface in the lives of your children for them to deal with.

A minister from Ghana once shared this testimony on T.D Jakes Men's Conference a while ago. By the time he attended the same conference the year before the testimony, he and his wife had separated. He then sought counsel from Bishop T.D. Jakes on this issue. He was advised to deal with the demon of divorce or his children would have to face it in the future.

This Ghanaian Minister then realised that indeed among his father's siblings, over thirty in number, they had all gone through one or more divorce by then. He quickly spent time before the Lord for a breakthrough and to the glory of God, by the time of his testimony, his wife and himself were back together.

At another time for whatever reasons, David refused advice and conducted a census that was displeasing to God. That brought about a plague in which 70,000 people died within hours. When he realised his mistake, he openly admitted responsibility for his sin, was willing to personally fall into the merciful hands of God, interceded for the people and gave to God a sacrifice that was costly to him. It was David that sinned yet it was the people that died! Every father/leader ought to be mindful of their decisions, as often times the innocent and vulnerable in the family or society end of paying for their mistakes. Equally, this should spur us to pray more for our leaders for godly directions and actions. Should there be a possibility that your wrong decisions expose your family or community to some sort of plague or any form of hardship, like David, confess your sins and give to God a worthy offering. In the multitude of counsellors there is safety *(Proverbs 24:6).*

Please pause and meditate on these songs:

Some common lyrics are:
Oh the blood of Jesus
Oh the blood of Jesus
Oh the blood of Jesus
It washes white as snow.

There's deliverance in the blood of Jesus
There's deliverance in the blood of Jesus
There's deliverance in the blood of Jesus
It washes white as snow.

There's power in the blood of Jesus
There's power in the blood of Jesus
There's power in the blood of Jesus
It washes white as snow.

The author of the music and lyrics of the Hymn, Oh, the Blood of Jesus, is anonymous.
Source http://www.demonbuster.com/bloodmidi.html

What Can Wash Away My Sin?

What can wash away my sin?
Nothing but the blood of Jesus;
What can make me whole again?
Nothing but the blood of Jesus.
Refrain

Oh! precious is the flow
That makes me white as snow;
No other fount I know,
Nothing but the blood of Jesus.
Refrain

For my pardon, this I see,
Nothing but the blood of Jesus;
For my cleansing this my plea,
Nothing but the blood of Jesus.

Refrain

Nothing can for sin atone,
Nothing but the blood of Jesus;
Naught of good that I have done,
Nothing but the blood of Jesus.
Refrain

This is all my hope and peace,
Nothing but the blood of Jesus;
This is all my righteousness,
Nothing but the blood of Jesus.
Refrain

Now by this I'll overcome
Nothing but the blood of Jesus,
Now by this I'll reach my home
Nothing but the blood of Jesus.
Refrain

Glory! Glory! This I sing
Nothing but the blood of Jesus,
All my praise for this I bring
Nothing but the blood of Jesus.
Refrain

Words & Music: Robert Lowry, in Gospel Music, by William Doane and Robert Lowry (New York: Biglow & Main, 1876).

Source http://www.cyberhymnal.org/htm/n/b/nbtblood.html

David left a legacy

While in the wilderness many who were displeased ran to him and he provided for them and trained them. He was wise in his dealings with the Philistines. In the time of war, he volunteered to go into the battle with the Philistine army who had accommodated him and his family while running away from King Saul who wanted to kill him.

David had a good desire to build a temple for God but was prevented by God. He however provided all the materials ready for the construction of the temple. He got the people motivated to support Solomon in the construction task.

The Bible does not say at which point David changed and took his fathering role responsibly but we do know that before he died:

- ❖ He provided the plans, materials and the people to help Solomon build the temple.
- ❖ He instructed Solomon and gave him the leadership manual.
- ❖ He told Solomon how to secure his kingship by telling him who to eliminate and quickly too *(Joab and Shimei – 1Kings 2: 1-9).*
- ❖ He fought all the known enemies and left Solomon with a peaceful empire. By the way the enemy / demon that you as the father refuse to deal with will invariably wait for your children.

The fact that David started as a poor father did not mean he ended that way. Father, there is hope for you too. You might have made mistakes including serious ones with your earlier issues/children like David did with Absalom, Adonijah, Amnon etc, but you still have an opportunity with your Solomon. Do something or all that needs to be done while you are still alive, breathing and in good health. God thinks generationally, so should you.

Many business empires have collapsed or folded up after the demise of the proprietor. Many inventions have not seen the light of day because the man with the knowledge had died half way into the project. Father/brother, may your testimony not be like that in Jesus name. Learn from such people. As early as possible, carry your wife and children along in your business/ work etc. They are not too young to learn or be involved. Please don't leave it till it is too late when the child would have chosen another career or vocation or is not interested. If your child is not particularly enthusiastic about being in the same profession as yourself, learn to love and respect your child's choice but give him all the support and your child can learn transferable skills by working alongside with you.

David left Solomon with a peaceful and prosperous empire and advised him on how to make his kingdom more secure. Brother/father what demon have you refused to deal with or not confronted? And you are leaving it for your children. Could it be the demon of fear, high or low blood pressure, sickness, disease, divorce, poverty and lack, unpaid debt, etc? Remember the demon you refuse to deal with or confront will confront your seed later.

It seemed physically impossible for Solomon to fail in his earlier years as his father's successor. Why? David provided all the material and human resources from within and outside with his foreign partners. Father, what plans have you provided such that none of your children fail as your successor? What investments are you leaving them should God call you home today? The Bible says a good man leaves inheritance for his grandchildren.

Children nowadays tend to grow and get bigger physically than their parents. We live today in a global village dominated by technology. The child's level of knowledge is vast but that does not mean that the child has more experience than the parents. Please teach and train your children to be streetwise. A preserved childhood is better than an amended adulthood.

Mind your business

David in running away from King Saul ended up living in the wrong place; among the enemies of Israel. In order to cover up his raiding activities he lied to his host and killed everyone so that none was alive to inform his host. Father, please be mindful where you choose to relocate in the midst of any impending danger as you might be exposing yourself and family to more dangers. Many are living in Sodom and Gomorrah, in the midst of sin and doing all that they should not do as children of God; compromising when and where they should not as they are in the wrong camp. In David and his men volunteering to fight alongside the Philistines, David would have found himself fighting King Saul his father in-law and benefactor and Jonathan his best friend. Thank God for His divine intervention that made them to send him back. Brother being in the wrong place if care is not taken can expose you to attacking and destroying important relationships and communities or even your roots.

David exposed his family and associates to danger whilst fighting other people's battle. There was no adequate protection or security for them. How many fathers today spend considerable time minding and mending other people's businesses while their own children, wife, family and business are suffering in the hands of the enemies of loneliness, harassment, abuse of all types, and enslavement to non-prescribed drugs, with their business suffering from inadequate or poor management, wasteful spending, unworthy business deals or ventures etc. Thank you dad for providing the financial and material resources but dad now is the time for you to return home, salvage your family from the claws of the enemy and protect them. It is time for you to take full control of your business too.

Women are intuitive

David's wife Michal informed him of a threat over his life and made plans for his escape. Although there was no visible confirmation at that time of the likelihood of his being sent for and killed by King Saul, it was good that David heeded his wife advice. Brother, God has placed in women intuition, the ability to smell, notice, sense or see impending dangers or evil long before most men do. Please do not disregard your wife's advance warning of any impending danger however spiritually way up you may be as this can mean life or death for you. At another time, Abigail spoke kindly to David and persuaded him not to avenge himself. This he did and the Lord fought and killed Nabal without him having to lay his hands on Nabal to kill him.

Fear none else but God

God made a covenant with David such that even though David appeared to have fought more battles than any other king, yet he was not overcome. God helped him to win all the battles. No one who rose against David lived to tell the story including Adonijah and Absalom his own children. Brother, learn never to fight against the anointed one or the one whom God has a covenant with for you will not win.

David was a man after God's own heart in spite of his many

sins. There is hope for you, dad and brother if you will truly repent of your evil and wicked ways before your creator and maker. Whose heart are you after? God's heart or are you after money, wealth, power or affluence?

The heart cry of many children could be summed up as follows:

Thanks dad for all the toys
but I need more of your time.

Thanks dad for all the gifts
but I need more of your training.

Thanks dad for all the clothes
but I need more of your warmth.

Thanks dad for all the trips abroad
but I need more trips to Church.

Thanks dad for my education
but I like to know more about God.

Perhaps you would like to say a prayer for yourself now that you have compared your life with David's life. You may wish to say a prayer like this:

Father, I come before You thanking You for the privilege of studying and understanding my life in the light of the life of David. I confess that

I had a poor, unhealthy and non-remarkable childhood. I feel even till now that I am being underestimated, undervalued, unappreciated, unloved and unwanted, but I choose from now to align my life with Your word. I confess that I am wonderfully, complexly and beautifully made.

In line with Your words I choose to forgive all who treated me badly in life especially when I was younger. (You might wish to name them.)

Father, I have sinned in many ways like David, in direct disobedience to Your words in the following areas (please feel free to mention all your sins here). In shame, I confess these sins which I have primarily sinned against You and Your people. I ask that in the name of Jesus Christ, I be forgiven, cleansed and restored. Please do not hold any of my sins against any of my children. Thank You Lord for answered prayers in Jesus' name I pray and with thanksgiving. See 1 John 1:8-9 and Psalms 51.

Chapter 3

THE FATHER WHO SUCCEEDED IN HIS CAREER BUT FAILED AT HOME.

The sound high priest

Eli was the high priest before the conception and birth of Samuel at Shiloh. To have been the priest in charge then he must have been a descendant of Aaron and was anointed for the position. See *Leviticus 21-22*.

Eli with the anointing of God on him, pronounced God's blessings on Hannah *(1 Samuel 1:17)* and so it came to pass. Eli constantly blessed Elkanah and Hannah whenever they came to offer the yearly sacrifice and worship after Samuel had been given to the Lord. In the end 'barren Hannah' became the mother of six including Samuel. Father, with God's anointing on you, bless your family and those you come in contact with.

The father in the home is meant to be the high priest of that home as Jesus is our High Priest in heaven. To be the high priest then called for a sound knowledge of God, a relationship with Him, worshipping Him correctly as written in *Leviticus 21-22*, performing all the necessary sacrifices of peace offering, atonement, etc.

Father, you are meant to be the high priest of your family, bringing your family to the Lord in prayers and worship, seeking the face of the Lord on behalf of your family and those you are responsible for. Your mandate requires you to be physically and spiritually clean, set apart for God's use to bless your family and mankind, in tune with God and hearing from God, applying the necessary corrections as and when required.

In *1 Samuel 1 12-16* Hannah kept praying to the Lord and from her heart not minding Eli's presence. Eli misunderstood and misjudged Hannah and he rebuked her. Eli was insensitive to Hannah's plight; he never asked what it was and just assumed she was drunk. 'Not so my lord, Hannah replied, 'I am a woman who is deeply troubled. I have not been drinking wine or beer; I was pouring out my soul to the Lord. Do not take your servant for a wicked woman; I have been praying here out of my great anguish and grief' *(1 Samuel 1:15-16).* Eli must have realised how wrong he was though he did not apologise to Hannah. Nevertheless God used Eli to pronounce a blessing on Hannah. 'Go in peace' *(1 Samuel 1:17).* It was in God's peace that Hannah received her miracle not in strife, anger, jealousy, bitterness etc. *(Psalms 46:10 –11; 2 Chronicles 20:15-17).*

** From "Provocation, Prayer and Praise"
by O. Ola - Ojo 2010.
ISBN 978-0-9557898-3-0 Used by Permission from Protokos Publishers, UK.

Eli accepted Samuel at a very early age; he fed him, tutored and mentored Samuel *(1 Samuel 2:18-20).* Eli could have told Hannah that he already has a complete family and so he didn't want another child to raise but he didn't. In God's calendar of events, God knew Eli's children will not be fit to take over from their father and He would need a prophet/priest for his people therefore the divine arrangement for Samuel to be born and live with Eli. Father, is the Lord prompting you to foster or adopt another child? Or sometimes for reason beyond any human explanation you have to raise your grandchild or grandchildren just like the maternal grandparents of President Obama (the first African-American President of USA) played a significant part in raising him. Challenging as it may be, if you will respond to God and that family or child heart's cries, God will help you raise that child up successfully. Eli knew God enough to recognise that God might be trying to call and speak to Samuel when Samuel heard his name being called in the night. He taught Samuel how to respond correctly to God's call even in the night *(1 Samuel 3:1-11).*

Eli did not envy Samuel for hearing from God nor get worried over the possibility of Samuel being the next Prophet of God over his sons nor used that as an excuse to mistreat or plan to kill Samuel.

Eli loved the ark of the Lord and he was very concerned for the safety of the ark when it was taken to war against the Philistines. The ark of the Lord signified the presence and power of the Lord. He fell from his seat and died as soon as he was told that the Philistines in a war had captured the ark of Covenant *(1 Samuel 4:11-18)*.

The apathetic father doesn't get his priorities right

The law of the land in many ways are trying to capture the presence and power of the Lord in our lives, families and society today. How are you as the father or brother reacting to such news e.g. banning public Christian worship, removing praying including the Lord's prayer and worship in our public schools, distributing condoms and morning after pills to the young children and teenagers at schools free of charge without parental knowledge or consent, lowering the age for homosexual relationships, campaigning for safe sex instead of no sex before marriage, granting adoption rights to homosexuals etc?

Eli's children disrespected God in their service in His household. They were ways away from their duties and perhaps were disconnected from God, perhaps they did not know God for themselves or perhaps felt that their father's godliness will substitute for their ungodliness. There could be many reasons why children of pastors and church leaders are slipping away from the Lord. These, unfortunately, could be because some:

- Fathers are rarely available because they are too busy in the church or mission field.
- Fathers come home only wanting to eat and sleep mostly.
- Fathers have not involved their children in praying or reading the word of God or observing specific prayer times.
- Fathers don't make time or spare the time to teach their children basic life skills, household stuff, school work or God's word let alone play with them or go on outings with them or date them.
- Fathers continuously criticise their children instead of encouraging or motivating them.
- Fathers have not intimated their children in family challenges and trials and engaged the children in praying together to see their prayers answered by God.
- Fathers have time for everyone else but their family.
- Fathers lives are in contrast with what they teach, preach or proclaim i.e. 'do as I say not do as I do' fathers. For example, do you teach or proclaim faith but in crisis times exhibit fear, wrong attitude and confession?
- Fathers are terrors to their children and are not so approachable by the children.
- Fathers give the impression that their children are burdens not blessings to them.

- ❖ Fathers focus on their birthmarks instead of teaching from their experiences or scars.
- ❖ Fathers do not teach their children how to be 'streetwise' in today's society.
- ❖ Fathers who tell 'half truths'.
- ❖ Fathers have treated their spouses badly including belittling and/or beating them.
- ❖ Fathers do not affirm or confirm their children's achievements however little.

Providing for the family by the father is all encompassing. It ought not to be limited to providing food on the table but include good and godly training, preferably, by example. A father ought to be there for the children while they are growing, be an essential part of their lives and challenges and spend quality time in bringing the children up in the knowledge of the word of God and prayers. It is good to be successful on the mission field or career but it is much preferred to be successful with your children and wife.

When Eli was warned of the coming danger i.e. the destruction of his sons by God, the Bible never said he tore his clothes let alone warn them or intercede on their behalf *(1 Samuel 2:27- 36, 3:11-18).* God usually reveals to redeem. God's revelation through the man of God and Samuel did not make Eli to intercede for his sons and family. The fact that God has said something which might be negative does not preclude you from seeking His face in prayers and worship like Hezekiah. The same God who says people are to die is able to make them live, just like the Israelites and Moses in the wilderness and the people in Nineveh.

Getting your children with you to church is something, but ensuring that the children are actually in the service during the time of service is another. Fathers like Eli are encouraged to ensure that their children are actually in the sanctuary or in the Sunday school at the appropriate time. Please teach and train your children not to become vile especially to God and the things of God. God judged Eli's sons because they were vile and Eli did not restrain them. *(1 Samuel 3:13).* The consequences for their sins included:

- ❖ No more automatic honour *(1 Samuel 2:27-30).*
- ❖ God refusing any sacrifice or offering to purge their sin *(1 Samuel 3:13-14).*
- ❖ No man was to live to an old age *(1 Samuel 2:31).*
- ❖ All the increase in his house to die in the flower of their age *(1 Samuel 2:33).*
- ❖ Priesthood and priesthood anointing removed from Eli's sons *(1 Samuel 2:35).*
- ❖ Abject poverty in the surviving family members making them to beg for bread. *(1 Samuel 2:36).*

Spend quality time dad teaching and training your children at home in all aspects of life not only on Biblical matters but also how the children can be 'streetwise'. Spend quality time dating your children; get to know them and their aspirations and struggles. Please be a blessing indeed at home to your family too. An elderly minister like William Carey recently said the recipe for success is for the father in the home to put God first, his family second and his vocation third. Please get your priorities right.

Unfortunately, it is not uncommon for young people born by Christian parents to want to or actually stray from God and the Church. Parents need to spend quality time before God interceding for their children especially when they might have strayed from the Lord or His commands. They also need to have quality time with their children when they can positively impart the love and fear of God into each child. No parent should fear any child enough that the child is not told the truth about God and what He expects of each child in the family. Abraham was a good example of an intercessor and so were Moses and Job. Please father, just like the father of the prodigal child didn't give up, don't give up but keep interceding for your children.

Just as it is not legal or right that a child uses his father's certificate to look for work, so it is clear that most positions in life are not hereditary or automatic or can be passed down, each person must work hard and earn the position. Salvation is personal. Eli's sons perhaps thought they will automatically become the high priests because of their birth and cared less about their character and conduct before God and man. God nevertheless had rejected them and looked for little Samuel whom He could trust. Parents ought to be aware of this fact when bringing up their children.

Parental discipline that is given late leads to heartbreak. Parental discipline that is never given leads to heartbreak and a 'neck break'.

Pastors and Ministers of the gospel beware; God expects you to train your children in His fear if the anointing for priesthood is to continue with your children. Being successful will not necessarily entitle your children to qualify for your anointing or God's appointment as your successor. Please learn from Eli and Samuel, great prophets of God and highly respected by men but whose children were disqualified to continue in the lineage of priesthood.

Perhaps you would like to say a prayer for yourself now that you have compared your life with Eli's life. You may wish to say a prayer like this:

> *Father God, thank You for reminding me that as a father, I am meant to be the high priest in my home. Of a truth Lord, I have missed the mark of this calling in view of my short comings such as (you may wish to name them). Father, I come to You confessing them all and thanking You for Your cleansing and my forgiveness as in 1 John 1:8-9. I need Your help to live a godly life, a life that reads Your Word, understands it, obeys it, teaches and lives by it.*

I need Your help in bringing our children up in the love and fear of the Lord so that each one of them will live by Your word and standard not by the standard of the world even when we as parents are not there to see what is going on.

Lord in Your mercy, please teach me how to socially engage our children and make me to be a positive influence in their lives so that they will grow up in Your house like Samuel, a pillar not a caterpillar (with its destructive tendencies) in Jesus' name I pray with thanksgiving. Amen.

Chapter 4

THE FATHER WHO SHOWED UNCONDITIONAL LOVE.

Luke 15:11-32.

Let your children self-express

One of the greatest hurts that any parent can experience is to have a child who is wayward, selfish or thoughtless; and inconsiderate of others. Children who bring sorrow or disgrace to the family perhaps because of their performance or total negligence of God or family values break their parents' hearts. Such children often move far away from the home as soon as possible and may not be easy to win back home again. Shouting, ranting and arguing may not bring them back home nor make them do as you say to them like in the years past. But from my experience, an unconditional love, a forgiving spirit, a prayerful and watchful father will make them want to come back home. Under normal circumstances, every child seeks the father's attention, wants to gain his approval and bask in his love. However, fathers who have neither provided the love, approval or attention may find their children not wanting to come back home once they have left their home. How much of your love, not money, time, not toys have you poured on your children that you are sure will enhance their return home?

This father in *Luke 15:11-32* had two sons, the obedient one and the fun seeking one. He gave birth to both sons. His older son suffered from the pride of life while the younger one suffered from the lust of the flesh (Galatians 5:16-21). Their loving father understood both children and was able to accommodate their personalities. He went out of his way to meet each of them at their points of weakness. *See verses 22, 28b, and 31.*

He was an immensely wealthy and generous man with many servants. Before him, each son had the freedom of expression. He gave freedom to his children without imposing his will on any of them *(verses 12-31).* Can you as a father say of a truth that there is freedom of speech or expression in your home or do you impose your ideas always on your family and everyone around you thus shutting everyone up verbally and not allowing them to express themselves? Except you allow children to freely express themselves, you are in danger of turning them unnecessarily into introverts and it will be difficult to know what is on their mind let alone correct them where they are wrong or encourage good thoughts and ambitions.

He never gave up on his wayward son: he daily and patiently waited for this lost son. Is there any of your children that you have given up on father, and why have you given up on that child or children? You might have invested so much of your time, life and resources and it does not seem like that child has turned out right in your sight but don't give up, they like you are under God's construction and He their maker has not finished with them. Prayerfully, with a heart of gratitude to God, wait for a turn around, a return home.

He only gave to the son who asked of him as seen in verses 12 and 29. How are you doing with giving to your family especially your children? You may give without loving but you truly cannot love your family without giving to them. What do you give dad, material resources or your time and talent? Who do you give to the most among your children; the one who keeps asking or the quiet one? You need to give your time to the child who asks but some children would just not ask, such children should be loved more and encouraged to ask. Are you fond of not keeping your promises or not pulling your financial weight in the home as a father? That might make your sensitive children not to ask you for help or things etc.

Many today will want to receive but without asking God. Others ask in unbelief. There is a place for unwavering faith and tenacity sometimes before you receive from God. If and when you refuse to ask from your Father, don't be jealous if others who ask God get blessed. God has never been and will never be too tired to answer you whenever, wherever and for whatever makes you want or need to call on Him.

The father was full of mercy and grace towards the wayward child. Children will always be children no matter what.

Allowances should be made for them when they have gone wrong to receive from you mercy, love and grace especially when they have retraced their steps to you. Nagging over the previous mistakes will create more gulfs between you, the father and the child than mend the broken relationships.

But when he was yet a great way off, his father saw him, and had compassion, and ran, and fell on his neck, and kissed him (see verse 20). A great way off, yet his father saw him! Why? Because he was very watchful and in his heart he knew his runaway son would return. He could be sure of his son's return because:

- ❖ He knew he had trained his son enough such that departing from his training and remaining in a strange land forever would be impossible.
- ❖ He knew he has shown his son so much love at home that couldn't be paralleled elsewhere. How much love have you shown your child that would make them come back home especially when they have ran into trouble? A song says 'the love He's shown couldn't make me think He'll leave me in trouble'.
- ❖ He knew his son was on a journey on the 'dead end' road and would soon realise it and retrace his steps back home.
- ❖ He knew the outcome of such demands by his experience of life – a life from home for his son could not be forever. An African adage says when the young people are cutting trees in the forest; the onlooking elders already know where the cut tree will fall. Age and experience in life gave him the ability of predicting the young man's return.

- ❖ He knew his son was sure of a place at home whenever he returned and that the young man would probably come back for his place at home.
- ❖ He knew he had an open and healthy communication with his son, though the son acted wrongly causing him some pains and shame, yet he did not curse him or disallowed him from going away to try the world nor did he tell him not to return once he left his home.
- ❖ He was a prayerful father who walked by faith and not by sight; he acted on his faith. Father, though your child is away in rebellion, lust or greed or sin, far away from home, please don't give up on him/her for your active faith will soon be rewarded.
- ❖ He knew his son enough to be able to predict him. Dad, how well enough do you know your child to be able to predict him or her?

He had compassion, and ran, and fell on his neck, and kissed him. He had compassion, not a mind of anger or revenge and he was not spiteful, judgmental or condemning. His assessment of his son from afar conveyed the hardship the young man had probably gone through. He couldn't wait for the son to get to him but ran to meet him. Christianity is about a loving Heavenly Father running in mercy through Jesus Christ to meet us in compassion. While in religion, mankind is seeking to get to God, in Christianity – a way of life, our Heavenly Righteous Father reaches out to draw us into His love and presence. He fell on his son's neck and kissed him. Dirty, tattered, unworthy of his love again and smelly as his son was, the father kissed the young man, gave him a warm welcome back home and a kind gesture he did not deserve. Salvation through the blood of Jesus Christ is not for the perfect human being but for the undeserving sinner like you and me. Every human being is so precious to God such that heaven rejoices when a lost sinner gives his or her life to Jesus.

But the father said to his servants, *'Bring forth the best robe, and put it on him; and put a ring on his hand and shoes on his feet'.* The father asked that the young man be clothed in the best robe available. God's love, like the snow, completely covers our sins and ugliness. He covered his son's shame and, ugliness from the onlooking world with the best robe available. Father do you expose your already week, feeble, dejected, ill, vulnerable child to the world or do you cover their shame in prayers, love, acceptance and provision?

The ring of authority given to the young man would have silenced all the enemies who might want to question his place again in the family perhaps and in the family business. It is possible that the young man had no shoes when he returned home or he had a well worn pair. Again to cover his son's shame and protect him he asked that the servant give him one.

You must be a good example

Is it not surprising that in spite of how this father had lived his life in the presence of his children, both did not take after him in most things? The younger one was selfish, lazy, and initially inconsiderate while the older one was lacking in mercy, full of bitterness, resentment, anger, unloving and thoughtless? Every father would love their children to emulate at least their good traits but what do you do if and when your children's behaviour and attitude are so divergent to yours? I suggest you keep living your righteous life trusting God to one day use same to reach out to your children.

The fact that your children have not turned out right once you have done your best as a godly parent ought, need not make you blame or harm yourself. The child that is of age who decides to run away from home will soon have himself/herself to blame. Although this may be a difficult period for you and the family, yet it is a time to look only unto God who is able to heal your wounds; emotionally, psychologically and spiritually, etc. Ignoring or denying the reality of the matter at hand won't make it go away.

The forgiving father

He saw his lost son from afar, ran to meet him, embraced him in love yet gave him the opportunity of open confession and apology. There is need for you to allow that child that has come back home, the opportunity to openly confess his/her sin and apologise to those whom have been wronged. There is healing in confession. *James 5:16* says *'confess your sins to one another and pray for one another'*. Remember *1 John*

1:8-10 too. There is a need and place for us to talk to God about our sins and come clean before Him, trusting Him for complete cleansing and restoration. He forgave the lost son and restored him to his position of sonship. After you might have disciplined that child, please dad, don't allow that child to go to bed without you restoring the relationship you have with them and without you showing the children that you love them though you hate their sin(s) or wrongdoing(s).

He threw a party for the homecoming of his lost son which was costly to him; materially and much more as it led to the killing of a fattened calf. Learn as a father to celebrate each achievement of your child or children, be it when they are taking their first steps, passing their examinations or repenting and coming back to the Lord; they are all worth celebrating. God the Father is very creative such that He has made no two people the same; even identical twins will exhibit some slight differences. He made the whole world from nothing and all the wealth on earth and in heaven is His. God the Father loves each person equally for in His presence we are the same and equal irrespective of our race, background, sex or our past. All have the freedom of speech and ability to approach Him anywhere and for anything. He is very accommodating of our weaknesses and failures. God the Father will never give up on the sinner whom He loves although He hates the sin and with Him there is always the opportunity of a second chance.

Redemption is very costly to God the Father. Nonetheless it has been well prepared for as Jesus Christ His only son had to die on the cross to pay the price of our sins *(see John 3:16)*. Much as God loves the sinner, salvation is by faith and the open confession of the faith. (see *Romans 10: 9-11 and John 3: 17-18)*. God the Father will give to **all** who will ask of Him yet He gives **all** the freewill to do as they like with such gifts. (see *Luke 19: 12-24)*. God the Father is still looking out for any sinner who will repent of their sins. He never gives up on any sinner and is always going out to meet each sinner (son) at their point of weakness. The living church of God must be concerned with the lost souls and actively look out for them, reach out to them, never give up on any one.

Father, how much do you know about your children; their likes and/or dislikes; what makes them happy or sad; what their goal in life is; how much do you understand each of your children and how able are you in accommodating their personalities? In what ways have you gone out of your way to meet each of your children at their points of weakness? Take time today parent and begin to get to know each of your children. This father came out to meet each child at his point of weakness and perhaps frustration, father please come out physically in acts of love and mercy and if you can't physically reach him/her then on your knees in prayers for your children at their time of weakness. Please, fathers remember that no child, however bad is beyond God's redemption.

*Most of what has been put under the father who showed unconditional love have been culled from 'Grace or Works' by O. O Ola -Ojo ISBN - 978-0-9557898-5-4.

Used by the permission of Protokos Publishers

Just before we end our looking at the life of the father who showed unconditional love, should you be a parent and one or more of your children have deliberately or otherwise walked away from home or from the godly faith in which you brought them up, I suggest that you say this prayer with me and mean it.

Dear Father,
Thank You for the opportunity that I have to read Your Word and see my life in the light of Your written and living word. Thank You for the privilege of parenting my children. (You might wish to name them) Thank You Lord for the children are Yours in the first instance and are uniquely made by You and for Your purpose.

Father, please I need Your help in understanding our child's/children's personalities and assistance in being able to accommodate their weaknesses and personalities. Please Lord, give me the wisdom and love to be able to reach out and minister to their needs. I need Your grace to forgive them when they go astray and Your Help to love them again in Jesus' name.

Lord, You know the pains and the agony of not knowing where my child is at present. I often feel that it's my fault for the way things are at present and do sincerely confess any of my known and unknown parental faults (mention or list them). Lord, I am concerned about my child's safety with the unknown friends in an unknown and unsupervised environment. Lord, please Help me not to give up on my child's safety and safe return home to us and to the gathering of believers. Lord please create in me in advance a loving and forgiving spirit full of mercy and grace, that equally allows me to be restored fully with my child. Help me Lord to lovingly support my child's return to Jesus Christ. Teach me, oh Lord, all that I need to be a living example of the parent You Lord created me to be.

I choose to forgive as many people who have wronged me in the process of this experience and also with Your help I choose to forgive myself.

Thank you Lord for yet another chance to experience Your love and once again be an example of a Godly parent. Please keep me, my wife and my children in the very hollow of Your Hands. Thank You Lord for everything in Jesus' name I pray with thanksgiving. Amen

Chapter 5

THE FATHER WHO HAD A FAVOURITE.

Isaac was born to elderly parents and into a wealthy family. His mother Sarah was 90 years old and his father Abraham was 100 years old at the time of his birth. His name means laughter and for as long as the parents were alive, he indeed gave them joy.

The trustworthy father

One day, his father took him and some servants and they travelled for some days to go and make a sacrifice *(Genesis 22:1-3)*. At the foot of the mountain, Abraham left his servants and took only Isaac with him to the top of the mountain Moriah *(Genesis 22:5-60)*. Isaac was old enough to carry the wood for the sacrifice and old enough to ask the father about the lamb for the sacrifice to which his father said the Lord will provide. *(Genesis 22:7-8)*. After the altar had been prepared, he could have ran away, however he allowed his father to lay him on the altar, bind him and raised his knife to kill him. He was so obedient unto death and also trusted in his earthly father *(Genesis 22:9-10).* God ultimately spared his life and indeed provided a lamb for the sacrifice. Isaac and Abraham were both able to return to the foot of the mountain to join with the servants and return to their home *(Genesis 22:11-19).*

Brother, how trusting are you in the Lord with regards to your life and committing all to Him knowing full well that your God is able to provide for all your needs? As Isaac laid down his life without struggling or trying to run away from his earthly father, how prepared are you to commit your life into God's hands trusting that He is able to give that same life back to you and with abundance *(Genesis 22:15-18).*

Isaac was forty years old when his father arranged for him to be married *(Genesis 25:20).* In *Genesis 24:1-10* Abraham put his house in order by sorting out all that getting a wife for his son entailed. Brother, should the family have to choose your wife for you perhaps according to your tradition even in this modern day, rather than rebelling against them, trust God and pray about all that this might entail so that you might end up with the right person to complement you for life. Isaac spent time alone on the field meditating before his bride arrived *(Genesis 24:62-65).* Brother, you need to spend time alone with God as you seek His face and wait for the right marriage partner.

Have you a wife or possession?

When he saw Rebecca, he loved her and took her into his mother's tent *(Genesis 24:6-67).* Brother, the Bible commands you to love the wife of your youth and be satisfied only in her *(Proverbs 5:15-19, Ecclesiastes 9:9 and Songs of Solomon 5:29).* Do you really love your wife for who she is – a child of God, created in God's own image and equipped to complement you *(Genesis 2:18–24)* or do you see your wife as part of your material possessions such as furniture to be used or abused and not loved? Do you compare your wife with other women? That is a recipe for disaster, downfall and disharmony in the home. Your wife is unique and has many godly traits and attributes if only you will take time to find out and encourage her in those positive traits. A man who loves his wife actually loves himself. It is in loving and praying for and with your wife that you stand to not only be blessed but to make her who you really want her to be.

When you want to be comforted or encouraged apart from God who or what do you turn to? Isaac was comforted by Rebecca when his mother went to be with the Lord. Love your wife enough so that she could understand you, your needs and be able to support you whenever and wherever there is a need or loss.

Isaac was a destiny carrier as the promises God made to his father was to continue with him *(Genesis 22:15-18).* Brother, have you realised how important you are in the agenda of God for your family and mankind? Do you realise you are a destiny carrier and that many generations yet unborn will have their life's affected by your relationship with God, your actions and lifestyle? It is time to begin to take stock of your life and see if it pleases God.

Isaac knew God for himself. Just as no one could eat for another person, Isaac had a personal relationship with God himself. First, he meditated alone in the fields whilst waiting for his bride, then he sought the face of the Lord on behalf of his wife for her barrenness and the Lord heard him and gave them twins *(Genesis 25:20-21).* Brother, do you have a personal relationship with God such that you can call on Him in times of your need? It was Rebecca that was barren, yet Isaac did not leave her to that problem or predicament alone, neither did he sleep with any other woman so that he could have a child but he prayed for her. Brother when last did you pray for and with your wife? It doesn't have to be because of barrenness but even for small problems. Whatever disturbs your wife in any way qualifies for your prayer and attention. Love your wife and take time to prayerfully lay hands on her too.

Dr. Gary Chapman said there are five love languages through which a person can communicate love with his / her spouse including:

- Affirmation by written or spoken words or actions.
- Performing acts of service including helping with house chores.
- Physical touching and cuddling.
- Giving gifts and presents.

- Spending quality time with your spouse.

Please brother, find out which of the love languages that suits your wife/spouse and use it

*http://www.garychapman.org/

Listen to your wife, women love men who find time to listen to their talks and concerns as they express them. You might not need to give any suggestion but listen to your wife, tenderly hold her, cuddle her and be expressive of your love to her in the way you know touches her most especially when she feels most vulnerable.

Add work to your riches

Isaac was born into a very wealthy family yet he worked. He re-dug his father's wells and gave them the same names *(Genesis 26:15-22).* Brother, that you are born into a wealthy family is not the reason for your not working or for being lazy. Riches don't stay in the family forever unless its source is nourished or looked after as riches can develop wings and fly away like a bird. You need to understand your riches and work more to make it yielding over the years. Isaac faced a lot of opposition as he dug the wells but he did not stop until finally he was able to say *'Now the Lord has made room for us and we shall be fruitful in the land' (Genesis 26:22).* There is wealth in the well. Brother, life is full of much opposition; winners don't quit and quitters don't win. If you do not quit in that which the Lord has given you to do, one day your victory over your enemies will come and you could say like Isaac that God has made room for you and you shall be fruitful in the land.

There is water, life and wealth in the well, whether it is water, mine, precious stones or oil well. The enemies put dirt in the wells and covered them up but Isaac changed location and re-dug the well knowing full well that there was good water flowing under the soil waiting to be tapped, waiting to be used. Isaac dug the wells and also gave them the same names as his father. God's blessings over your life are without repentance. You might need to change location and dig the well into your abundant life. The well you need to dig might an idea God revealed to you earlier but you have long forgotten, a family business, a profitable past-time, God-glorifying hobby etc. Brother, whatever it is, I challenge you in the name of the Lord to rise up and dig the well again and regardless of whatever opposition the enemy might be putting on your way. Be encouraged to re-dig the well again.

Isaac sowed in the time of famine and in the same year the Lord gave him a hundred-fold return. Isaac sowed by faith when it did not seem logical to sow – a famine time, difficult time, hardship time. Isaac used water from his well to irrigate his farm whilst the Philistines depended on rain drops. With God's blessing, whilst draught destroyed the Philistines crops, his crops were flourishing and blossoming. Brother, ask for a divine revelation for the technique or the technology that would help you to increase your productivity at work and at cheaper rate than using the conventional method. It is always better and more profitable to be ahead of technology in your calling. *'The Lord blessed him and the man became rich; he prospered more and more until he became wealthy. He had possession of flocks and herd, and a great household so that the Philistines envied him' (Genesis 26:12-14).*

Sow your best seeds

What do you sow brother into the work of the Lord and the life of others? The best or the worst seed? What do you sow into your time of fellowship with God? The best time of your day or the left over i.e. the end or tiring minutes of the day? What you sow determines your harvest; a habit of a one-minute prayer time and Bible study time cannot be expected to produce great results as waiting before the Lord would. 'Whatsoever a man sows, that will he reap'.

Brother, the Lord has given you two types of seed from your harvest which might just be your income or farm yield – one type of seed is for eating and the other type of seed is for sowing. Do not attempt to eat all of your harvest for there will not be any left to sow. Many are yet to understand the principle of tithing - it is the seed that you sow in obedience to God and for your own protection and future provision. How many have kept putting off paying their tithes and yet are not financially balanced, getting into one form of trouble or the other that takes away their savings, peace, health, inheritance and blessings. Your tithes belong to God and must be given to Him as the first fruit before you touch the rest of your income or harvest. (*Malachi 3:8-9*).

Isaac sowed when it was most inconvenient – in famine time, a time others would have hoarded what they had, yet the Lord looked down on the seed sown and gave him a hundred fold return! (*Genesis 26:12-14*). The God of Isaac is alive and well and He can be your God too if you have not asked Him into your life yet. He is still in the business of blessing the seeds sown in famine and giving a hundred or more return. Someone once suggested that if what you have is not enough to meet your need then sow it prayerfully and see what God can and will do. It really does not have to be money, you could sow a seed of your time into God's work or other people's life if that is all that you have and in due time God will reward you. Famine does not necessarily mean lack of food although it could be that, it could also be famine relating to lack of good health or the fruit of the womb or a good job or career etc.

Loving and giving go together

Do you give from your abundance or happily share the little you have with others? You may give without loving but you cannot truly love God or any other human being without giving; love and giving go together. True love always seeks to give. How do you react to the call to give in the household of faith or in your family or to the less privileged around you? You can justify your actions but God is looking for your motive.

Abel was preferred to Cain on account of his sacrifice to God. Will God prefer someone else to you on account of your giving to the Lord? It's not by the size of your offering but on your motive and sincerity.

Isaac before he died pronounced blessings on his sons. He was tricked by Rebecca and Jacob to give Esau's blessings to Jacob but nevertheless he blessed Esau *(Genesis 27:1-40).* No one knows the time of death, brother please make it a daily habit to bless your family. There is anointing and life in your tongue.

History repeating itself

Isaac like his father lied about the identity of his wife because of the fear of the Philistines whom he thought may take his wife and kill him. *(Genesis 26:6-11).* Isn't it strange that Isaac repeated his father's lies though he was not yet born by the time Abram lied regarding Sarai his wife!

Abraham waited for 25 years before Isaac was born. Isaac waited for 20 years before his twins were born. Jacob waited many years before Rachael his beloved wife had any child. When and where a bad history is repeating itself in your family, please take time to seek the face of the Lord for victory.

Do not permit favouritism in your home

Isaac allowed favouritism in his home *(Genesis 25:24- 28)*. Though blessed with a set of twins, Isaac chose to love Esau their firstborn whilst Rebecca loved Jacob their younger son. In a family of four, there were at least three cooking pots, one for Esau, one for Jacob, one perhaps for Isaac and Rebecca *(Genesis 25:29 –34)*. Brother, each child God gives to you and your wife is unique and is to be loved not more or less that the other siblings. Favouritism in the home is the number one sure recipe for disunity, envy, jealousy, unnecessary fighting amongst siblings and if care is not taken, killing one another *(Genesis 37:3,19-20)*. *Favouritism can blind the eyes of the parents to the good traits of their other children. It can make the unfavoured child angry, disobedient and rebellious. The favoured child gets exposed and becomes vulnerable to the other children.

Just before we end our looking at the life of Isaac, may we pray together please?

> *Father in heaven, thank You for allowing me to see a reflection of my life through the life of Isaac. I confess that I am a blessed child, loved by You and in this world to bring godly laughter to all I come in contact with.*

Father, I confess my sins of not loving my wife enough and/or comparing her with others, not listening to her enough and not praying for her. Please Lord, forgive me and help me in the following areas (you might wish to list them).

Father, I confess my sins of showing favouritism with my children and ask that You please forgive me. Just as You love me like any other person that You have created, please teach and help me on how to show a balanced love in my family from now on in Jesus name. Our children are blessed of and by God and are highly favoured. I choose with God's help to daily bless them as from now in Jesus name. (you may wish to list their names here)

Father, I openly acknowledge and confess not paying my tithes and/or giving good offerings to You as expected especially not bringing it as the first fruit. I confess I have not given enough to Your work or and to others in need. I also confess the times when due to famine or poverty around me, I did not sow, out of fear for the present and future, out of selfishness and greed and out of lack of love. Please forgive me and help me to give from now on especially in times of famine and hardship.

Father, I bring before You areas of famine in my life, family, church, loved ones (you might wish to list their names here) and I ask You to please help me as I sow by faith into these areas. I trust You for a hundred fold on this seed as I sow it in Jesus' name. Thank You Lord for answered prayers in Jesus' name I pray with thanksgiving. Amen.

* Taken from 'To the Bride With Love'
by O. Ola-Ojo ISBN978-0-9557898-4-7
Used with the permission of Protokos Publishers.

Chapter 6

THE FATHER WHO GOT PAID IN HIS OWN COIN.

Favoured from the womb

Esau and Jacob were non-identical twins conceived as a result of a praying father. However from the womb, God chose Jacob over Esau *(Genesis 25:21-23, Malachi 1:2-3, Romans 9:10 –16).* Why this was so, we can't tell. Jacob was their mother's favourite, he was a good cook and a quiet man living in tents. *(Genesis 25:27-28).*

Brother, out of God's own mercies, He has chosen you above many others who perhaps are more intelligent, powerful, handsome, more knowledgeable etc. The very fact that you were conceived, born alive and have lived to read this book is confirmation of God's special choice of you. Perhaps I should remind you that there was a possibility of another sperm fertilising your mothers's egg but among over potential several thousands of other sperms, yours was the one that made it quickest and strongest to fertilize your mother's egg in her womb. God loved you enough to personally supervise your formation and growth in your mother's womb *(Psalms 139:16).*

Jacob with his good cooking skills took Esau's birthright from him with a bowl of pottage, lentil and bread *(Genesis 25:27-34).* He grabbed Esau's heel on the way out of their mother's womb and now he cunningly took Esau's birthright from him.

Jacob obeyed their mother in deceiving their father Isaac, thereby collecting the blessings of the first born instead of Esau. He initially protested but went along with their mother's plan thereby receiving Esau blessings *(Genesis 27:1-29).*

When Esau found out what Jacob had done, he planned to kill Jacob after their father's death and their mother Rebecca convinced their father of Jacob's need to visit his uncle Laban in order to get a wife. Jacob in obedience to his parents therefore had to leave home because of this *(Genesis 28:10–17).*

Angels standing by

On his way to Uncle Laban, he slept in the night and there God appeared to him in a dream. He saw angels climbing the ladder to heaven and coming down from heaven. Care must be taken as we have all around us angels who take our thoughts and confessions to God and subsequently descend with answers to our prayers, thoughts and confessions. Brother, God is willing to reveal Himself to you anywhere and at anytime if you will only key into loving and worshipping Him.

Dreaming uncommon dreams

Dreams often give guidance, direction, confirmation, clarity, correction into our future. Jacob's dream was not an ordinary dream. Jacob realised that and acted accordingly. Many times God will reveal a situation or the future to His children. What we do to such dreams is important. Dreams that come from God if acted upon in a godly way will bring peace and joy and will come to pass bringing God the glory and to the recipient victory, blessing, accomplishment and joy.

It will always be in line with God's words e.g. Daniel's dream in *Daniel 7:1-15.* Pharaoh's dream in *Genesis 41:1-36*, Joseph's dream in Matthew 1:18-21, Peter's dream in *Acts 10:9-23,* Nebuchadnezzar's dream in *Daniel 2:1-49, 4:1 – end* and John's dream in *Revelations 1:1.*

Waking up from this dream, Jacob built an altar unto the Lord and poured oil on it and made a vow to the Lord *(Genesis 28:18-22).* He subsequently redeemed his vows and built more altars unto God in worship *(Genesis 35:1).* What vow have you made to God or man? Have you redeemed the vow - yes or no? if no, why not? Be prudent and sincere when you to make vows especially to God.

Marriage, at what price?

Jacob invariably met his cousin Rachel at the well when he came to the land of the people of the East and he helped her. He instantaneously fell in love with her and when asked later by Uncle Laban what his wages would be for looking after his flock, he said he would serve Uncle Laban for seven years in return for Rachel's hand in marriage *(Genesis 29:1-20).* Jacob was hard working and in all the years of his faithful service unto his uncle, he did not molest Rachel nor take advantage of her. What price have you paid or are you willing to pay for your wife, brother? We live in a fast world, much faster than our fore-fathers, a world where people do not hesitate to take advantage of one another, a world where lots of people believe in instant gratification and the immediate satisfaction of self-interests and desires, a world where people live their lives directly opposite to the word of God, thinking they are smarter than their creator. Many marriage beds have been defiled on this account and there is cheap relationship, cheap sex, cheap marriages no wonder such cheapies don't last!

As a father, what bridal price have you or will you be asking your son-in–law or his family to pay in return for your daughter's hand in marriage? A man who is unwilling to pay or make a sacrifice for the sake of marriage in one form or the other may not be qualified to be your daughter's wedded husband. He sure must be able to prove himself and his character that he is capable of providing and caring for her at all times before she marries him. If you give your daughter to a man who has not proved himself worthy, you might have to be a father to your grandchildren. If you allow your son to marry a woman who has not proved herself worthy, you might have to be a mother to your grandchildren.

Good negotiating and creative skills

Jacob had good negotiating skills. First he used his skills to take the birthright from Esau his older brother in (*Genesis 25:29–34)*, then he used it to negotiate twice for marrying Rachel in (*Genesis 29:15-18, 25-28)* and at another time in negotiating his way of raising his flock from Laban's *(Genesis 30:25–36)*. Jacob was mindful of providing for his family and sought ways of meeting his obligations as a father and husband of four wives *(Genesis 30:30)*. Brother, how well are you into providing for your family including making sure they will be comfortable should the Lord decide to call you home now? Jacob was very creative, hard working and smart in the way he raised healthy flocks from Uncle Laban's flocks. (*Genesis 30:37–43)*. This he attributed to divine revelation from God. Divine revelation from God when obeyed always brings prosperity.

Return to your homeland

Jacob heard from God when it was time for him to return to his homeland. (*Genesis 31: 1-3)*. Perhaps, brother, you have been in a foreign land far from home for whatever reasons, it is best to wait until you hear from God before you make the move into trying to return home. God's time is the best, perfect and in His own agenda for your life will tell you when it is best for you and your family to return to your homeland.

Returning to his homeland was daunting for Jacob especially with his past of deceiving his father and brother whom he now had to face. Many stay abroad because of what they did before they left and because of who may be waiting for them at home.

Facing up to your past

Jacob initially was afraid to meet Esau on his way back home knowing full well how much he had hurt Esau. He made plans to appease the anger of his older brother by sending ahead of him gifts, and he approached Esau with respect and humility like many today who seek the favour of those whom they have offended with many presents.

It was time for Jacob to face the past that he had been running away from. A time to either pay the full price for his calculated cheatings and hurt inflicted on Esau or a time to find his favour and peace *(Genesis 32:1- 21).* How far have been able to run away from your unconfessed past? For how long brother will you continue to run from the rewards of your past life? It is time to own up to God and to those you have offended- trusting God to help you in this matter. A man's gifts will make room for him – gifts as in talents used properly, gift as in giving

- finding favour for when a man's way pleases the Lord, He makes his enemies to be at peace with him *(Proverbs 16:7)*. God's favour will take you past where your gifts can ever take you.

Broken before God

After sorting things and his family out as best as he knew to, he remained alone in the camp at night, there a man fought with him all night. There comes a time and a place brother where you alone get to and it is in that place of solitude that God will again show up so that he might change you and bless you.

Jacob had to be confronted with his past life of cheating others out of their rightful possessions, living up to his non-God glorifying name and coming into contact and covenant with his maker and God. He had to be broken before the Lord could use him. He had to come to the point of helplessness and hopelessness. He had to come to the point of acknowledging his need to be blessed by God than doing it his own way. Jacob was to inherit Abraham's blessings. It was a covenant blessing not an acquired blessing by cheating or scheming. God had to teach him that. His personal encounter with God this time around left him with a scar, limping and needing to depend on God from them on. 'Not by power, not by might but by My Spirit says the Lord' *(Zachariah 4:6)*. If he had banked on running should Esau try to kill him, he could no longer do so as one of his legs had been knocked out of the joint by the angel. Jacob made it right with Esau his twin brother after many years of separation. It is possible that by the time Esau met Jacob later, Esau felt compassion for his limping brother and must have thought Jacob with his limping leg could no longer pose a threat to him. What he failed to realise was that Jacob might be limping physically but he was a giant before God.

You must now face your past, my brother, without gimmicks or scheming; regardless of your independence or connections showing your total dependence on God your maker, the only One who declares victory before the battle.

Whilst the angel was in a hurry to leave after the fight with Jacob, Jacob would not leave the angel alone until he got the blessings he demanded of the angel. There is a place and time for everyone to tarry before God, holding on to His promises until one receives all that God has promised them and their household *(Genesis 32:24–28).* The angel did not give Jacob money or wealth on the spot but he changed his name from Jacob the grabber to Israel 'one who prevails with God and therefore will be able to prevail with men'. A good name is to be preferred to riches *(Proverbs 22:1).* God gave Jacob a second chance with his new name; with this he could put his past behind him and walk in the newness of his new name and relationship with God and people.

Wisdom by experience

Knowledge can be acquired but the best wisdom is by experience. A scar was left to remind him of the experience. A scar in itself doesn't hurt but it shows that there has been a fight, surgery or accident there before; in order words, there is a story to tell or an encounter to relate with every scar. Jacob's scar made his descendants not to eat that part of the joint till today *(Genesis 32:24-32).* Brother, don't waste or hide your experience, tell it to your family, friends and whosoever will benefit from it.

Many are born with conspicuous birthmarks due to no fault of theirs or their parents. It is many times circumstantial. A scar is acquired as one walks through life. A birthmark talks of where you are from but a scar talks of where you have been. No one has control over the birthmark e.g. choice of your biological parents, your hometown, place of birth, race or nationality, height etc. but with the scar, it may signify where you deliberately have been or forced to be.

Jesus Christ was born by poor parents and in a stable wrapped in a manger; his parents were so poor that at His presentation to the Lord after the days of Mary's purification were over, they brought a pair of turtle doves or two young pigeons *(Luke 2:21-24)* and He grew up to be a carpenter's son. That was His birthmark but it did not prevent Him from becoming who God wanted Him to be: the King over Israel and the Saviour of the world.

Boys talk about their birthmarks but men talks about their scars. Brother, it is time you stop talking about your birthmark but concentrate on talking about your scar and what the Lord has brought you through. Share the testimony of your scar to shame Satan and bring glory to God.

Hold on until you are blessed

A woman of God once said when God wants to bless a man, God will give the man a new name, resources and knowledge. God gave resources to Jacob whilst he was with his uncle Laban, he who went to Uncle Laban a bachelor with the barest property – some oil, a rod and perhaps a few clothes *(Genesis 28:18-19),* returned with great wealth and people as the Lord who promised him these on his way to Uncle Laban kept to His promises *(Genesis 28:11-18).* Whatever God has promised or is promising you brother is settled, for God does not speak any careless words *(Psalms 12:6).* Jacob gained his wealth and resources from Laban through divine revelation *(Genesis 31:1-13).*

Importance of a good name

Jacob knew the importance of a good name. He possibly realised how much a name could affect a person. As Rachel was dying in childbirth she named their son Ben-oni – meaning son of my sorrow of but Jacob quickly overruled and named him Benjamin *'son of my right hand' (Genesis 35:16-20).* Father, don't acknowledge what Satan is trying to do in your family but focus on the name of Jesus and what that name is capable of doing.

Brother, what is your name, the ones given to you from birth or the ones you have acquired over the years that is not God glorifying? Ask God for a new name. Your destiny might have been hidden or pronounced through your name. Learn to discard any non-God glorifying or edifying name- Who knows, perhaps that is all that you need to get into your destiny.

Jacob in love adopted Joseph's sons giving them the full rights like his other sons; he blessed them and most of his sons on his deathbed *(Genesis 48:1-21, 49; 1-28).*

The habit of sowing and reaping

The saying *'like father like son'* was so evident in the family of Jacob. Jacob as his name was, cheated on his twin brother twice, on their father by pretending to be Esau and on Laban by the way he raised his own flock from Laban. However God caught up with him through his sons. Fathers, be careful of what seeds you deliberately sow for you shall reap it's fruit in due season. For as long as the earth remains, there will be seed time and harvest time *(Genesis 8:22).*

Jacob had been chosen and favoured by God since in utero yet instead of leaving God to bless him, he cheated, possibly with the thought that he was helping God. His cheating led to his premature separation from his parents; he was all alone in the wilderness on his way to Uncle Laban and it would appear that their mother died before his return from Uncle Laban. Father in what ways have you been trying to help God? Cheating is definitely not the option. Now is the time for you to repent before it is too late.

Jacob favoured Rachel over Leah. The result of this was bareness and strife for Rachel and lack of love for Leah. This led to Leah and Rachel giving Jacob their maidservants to sleep with. He ended up with four wives! There is a saying in one of the Nigerian languages that 'one wife one trouble' you can imagine what it would have been like to have four wives at the same time!

Jacob took the birth right of the Esau and his blessings. He was advised to go away to Uncle Laban to avoid his twin brother's revenge. For over twenty years he was physically separated from his parents. Many years later, his sons pulled the rug from under him by lying that Joseph, the apple of his eyes, was probably torn by wild animals. Jacob believed his sons and lived in a lie for the next twenty two years as he was separated physically from Joseph his favourite son and worst still, he mourned over Joseph whom he believed was dead! Jacob's Abrahamic blessings could not immune him from reaping the reward of his previous sinful lies and deceits. For forty years plus, Jacob was separated from those whom he loved dearly. Let us be careful for we shall reap the reward of what we sow!

Avoid favouritism

Jacob also showed favouritism among his sons, choosing Joseph above his brothers and publicly displaying this by giving him the coat of many colours. Favouritism can easily destroy any home; it is to be avoided in the interest of peace and progress both for the individual members of the home and for the family in general. It is better to acknowledge the area of strength in each child than have a single favourite. For example, in my family we have the person who is best in good leadership skills, very accommodating, tolerant, has everyone's best interest at heart, is poised and committed to unity within the family even if it means giving up certain rights and comforts. There is another person who is best when it comes to accounting, forward planning, money matters and another person who is the link in the family ensuring everybody is fine and knows about what is happening to the rest of the family at any point in time etc.

What, you've got a foreign god!

Unknown to Jacob, Rachel had stolen her father's gods when they were leaving. When Laban came after him demanding for these gods, Jacob mistakenly cursed Rachel as he was unaware of the gods or the fact that the gods was among his belongings. In times of uncertainty, father, please and please again, it is better not to talk than speak any curses *(Genesis 31:31-32).* There is life and death in your tongue and as a father, God has given you authority over your wife and children. Please be careful how you use this power through your tongue.

Speaking curses need to be avoided by the father by all means, at all times, even when he is under an enormous pressure. Rachel, his beloved, never made it back to Canaan for she died on the way following Benjamin's birth.
The 'blame game' has been around since the days of Adam and Eve *(Genesis 3:10-13),* father have you come to the point where you can face up to your responsibilities or are you still apportioning blames?

As a father:

Who do you blame when things go wrong?
Who do you blame in the time of failure or adversity?
Who do you blame when things don't go on as planned?
Who do you blame when there is a loss in your own family?
Who do you blame when you can't explain what is going on?
Who do you blame when you end up being in the wrong place?
Who do you blame when you end up doing or saying the wrong thing?

Please do not curse

Whilst Jacob was on his deathbed, he blessed most of his sons but cursed some of them. *Genesis 49:5-7, James 3:10-12* says *'from the same mouth come blessing and cursing, my brother and sisters, this ought not to be so'.* Father, your last right is important and in your mouth is the power of life and death. Please avoid cursing any of your children or future generation for the cost is too much. The tribe of Levi lived under Jacob's curse until when they fought the Lord's battle *(Exodus 32:21-29).*

If perhaps you have been cursed, take it to the Lord in prayer. When you give your life to Jesus Christ, He will take away all curses from you and you no longer need to live a day under any curse *(Proverbs 26).*

Just before we end our focus at the life of Jacob, may we pray together please?

> *Dear Father in heaven, thank You for allowing me to evaluate my life in the light of Jacob's life. Father I humbly confess my sins for the times when I had thought I was smart like Jacob and Zacchaeus but cheated others of their inheritance, (please list them). I ask for your forgiveness and mercy in Jesus' name.*

For the times I have shown favouritism in my family, amongst my friends and associates, I ask you dear Lord to please forgive me in Your mercies. Help me from now to learn to be kind to all whom I will meet and be fair to all especially to my family members and associates.

Father, I bring before you this unfavourable family history that has or wants to repeat itself in my life (please list them). I come in the name of Jesus asking for total victory for myself and my generations to come, I confess Your words that says (insert your found scriptures here) and I boldly stand and declare that only the counsel of God shall stand in these matters.

For the vows I made to You or any man that I have been able to redeem, I give You Praise. For the following outstanding vows (you may list them here). I ask for Your help and grace to fulfil them.

Lord, You and I know this past (tell it to Jesus), which I have been running or trying to run away from. I realise that in order for me to enter into my inheritance for me in You, I need to face it, deal with it and conquer it. Lord I am afraid (list all your fears) but I come to You in Jesus name asking you to please help me, forgive me and bless me indeed. Lord, please change my name so that I may bear Your name alone from henceforth. Give me the wisdom and favour in dealing with this past in Your own way in the name of Jesus. Lord, please grant that my ways may please You as from now in Jesus name I pray and with thanksgiving. Amen.

Father I apologise for cursing the following people unnecessarily (name them). I repent of this wrong and I apply the Blood of Jesus to neutralise the curses in Jesus name. From now help me Lord to daily pronounce Your blessings as written in Your word on those whom I have previously cursed in Jesus name I pray and with thanksgiving. (Amen).

FACING THE PAST

What can be more disturbing for anyone
Than to have to face difficult situations.
Which they thought they had totally overcome
By their departure or change of environment.

Moses for fear of being killed for the Egyptian he murdered
Ran away to the land of Midian and stayed there with Jethro's family

For forty years he lived in Midian shepherding and raising a family
Alas God called him to return to Egypt and face Pharaoh.
Jonah in disobedience boarded a ship to Tarshish
Thinking he had been able to evade God's missionary call to Nineveh.
Later landed in the sea inside the belly of a big fish for three days and nights
He ended up on the shore of Nineveh, the town he was trying to run away from.

Joseph's brother in jealousy sold him to the Midianites
For over a decade they assumed they had got rid of him and his dreams.
Their trips during the famine years later brought them to Joseph.
The reality of which left them in constant fear of Joseph for as long as they lived.

For Joseph himself, the reunion with his brothers was traumatic too.
In love, he forgave them of their wickedness and plot to kill him.
He decided to look at the good their evil had brought him and the world
And he made adequate provision for the clan's resettlement in the best land.

For Paul the persecutor of the Church of God
His mission to Damascus changed his life and calling
No longer an accuser of the brethren but a brother and friend
He had to live to face the many threats of the Jews

Beloved today you might have to face the long forgotten Pharaoh or situations
That part of your life which you will want to and hope that people forget
Be assured God is able to turn your ungodly fears into godly faith
Your failure to fulfilment and mistakes to miracles

Your part of being able to face this very past situation
Depends on your forgiveness of the past no matter what
Your dependence on God for all that He will require of you
For you to be a winner you have to boldly face the past situation.

Chapter 7

THE FATHER WHO MADE THE COSTLY VOW.

(Judges 11-12)

A conspicuous birthmark

Jephthah, a mighty man of valour, was born by a harlot to Gilead, a man who had his own wife and other children. When the legitimate children grew up, they drove Jephthah out saying he would not inherit from their father as he was from a strange woman *(Judges 11:1-20).*

A wise person once said there is no an illegitimate child but an illegitimate father. Your birth circumstances or birthplace may be likened to a *'birthmark'* which is not within your control but it must not be allowed to dominate your life.

Jesus was born in a manger yet He is the King of kings and Lord of lords and the Saviour of the world. He did not allow His humble, unremarkable beginning or 'birthmark' to distract Him or prevent Him from reaching His calling and mission for the world.

The fact that you were born in the garage or in the taxi does not make you a taxi driver or a car, neither does being born in prison make you a prisoner, etc.

Brother, that you were picked up from the bin, born by a prostitute, etc. should not be treated more than you will treat or overlook a birthmark. When the devil or his emissaries want to remind you of your birthmark, remind them of your glorious destiny in life.

Disowned and driven out

Can you imagine being driven out of your father's home, comfort, protection and provision by your half brothers and not for any wrong doing but for being born by a harlot! While it was not Jephthah's fault to have been born by a strange woman, he was being punished for a sin which was out of his own control by his own half brothers.

Were you born physically out of wedlock and therefore have been prevented from your earthly inheritance? Cheer up for there is a better hope for you in Christ. In the eyes of the people - your family and associates - you might be referred to as illegitimate and so miss out on some things but in the eyes of the Almighty God, you were not an accident that happened but a person God planned and ordained to be born by your parents that way. God has a beautiful plan for your life which God in His time will unfold. God loves you just the way you are, you are precious in His sight. Perhaps you were born with a congenital condition that physically or medically puts you in a lesser position than your other siblings? Cheer up, the Lord who allowed the man to be born blind knowing full well that the blind baby will receive his sight in his adult life is still on the throne with regards to your incapability.

For men who think they should sow a seed everywhere they have visited, please rethink the repercussion this may bring to the innocent child conceived out of wedlock. You will definitely need to provide in advance a comfortable care package for the child's upbringing. You should see to it that you include them in your will.

Jephthah fled for his life and lived in the land of Tob where he learnt to fend for himself. His family might have rejected him but he kept going, fending for himself. There is an adage in one of the Nigerian languages which says, *'the person who denies you of your right or deliberately hurts you equips you with greater strength'* – *"adani l'oro f'agbara k'oni"*. Many of the worthless men rejected by the then society came to him and requested his leadership over them and he did so showing he had some leadership skills when he conquered the Ammonites. Jephthah could have kept away from everyone in his situation but he chose to help others like him. It was possibly easier for Jephthah to welcome, accommodate and train vain men, the rejects of the society for he knew what it felt like to be rejected. In the process, he sharpened his fighting and leadership skills.

What has made you flee from your father's home and where are you dwelling now? With the same accusation the devil has used against you, if you would turn it over to God, he would use same to work for you and to your own advantage. Believe it or not, whatever God has saved or delivered you from equips you better to help others in your former shoes. A saved prostitute is more likely to win more prostitutes, a saved thief, burglar or liar knows better how and where to get his former colleagues, a saved wife or child beater is in a better position to understand the reason and rationale for such behaviours and help those struggling with such behaviours, an ex-convict is more likely to get his mates to listen to his testimony. You catch my drift. This actually is the principle employed by the Full Gospel's Business Men's Fellowship worldwide founded by Demos Shakariahs.

They will be back

In the process of time, there came a war between the people of Israel and the children of Ammon. It then dawned on the elders of Gilead that the person they needed was Jephthah who had previously been driven out and was now residing in the land of Tob. The elders left Gilead and came looking for Jephthah to come and rescue them from their enemies. Where were these same elders when Jephthah was being driven out of his father's inheritance by his half brothers?

Isn't it strange how you are contacted by those who had previously abused, mistreated or abandoned you but now in their time of trouble especially when they think or know you are now in a position to help them out? Perhaps those who never or hardly contributed to your progress in life now want to cash in on your achievements! They now want to be associated with you who once they had despised, rejected, maltreated or abandoned! In certain cultures, illegitimate children are the sole responsibility of their mothers, however when such children grow up with astonishing achievements, the never-seen or known father shows up and may try to claim the achievement as his doing!

'And it came to pass in process of time, that the children of Ammon made war against Israel. And it was so, that when the children of Ammon made war against Israel, the elders of Gilead went to fetch Jephthah out of the land of Tob: that we may fight with the children of Ammon. And Jephthah said unto the elders of Gilead, Did not ye hate me, and expel me out of my father's house? And why are ye come unto me now when ye are in distress? And they said unto Jephthah, 'Come, and be our captain that we may fight with the children of Ammon.'

It was now time for Jephthah to make a demand from the elders from Gilead. His price for helping them out was for him to be made the captain and head of the whole town to which the elders consented *(Judges 11: 9-10)*. Isn't it strange that instead of Jephthah sharing out of his father's inheritance, he now was to be the captain and head of the town! Jephthah's testimony could be summarized like Joseph's – what his half brothers meant for evil, God meant for good *(Genesis 50:20)*. His mission in life now became obvious – he was to save and preserve the lives of the people of Gilead from their enemies. May I ask you brother, what is your assignment or mission in this life? Have you found it yet? If you know it, what are you doing with it? God makes no mistakes or rejects. He has a mission for all He has made, including you, brother. Equally you may have to name your price.

Jephthah like Joseph did not allow his painful past to stand in his way of helping the same people who once drove him out of his inheritance. Brother, now that the Lord has blessed you and lifted you above your enemies, rise up in the name of the Lord, forget the past, press on to the high calling of God for your life *(Philippians 3:13)*.

Know your history

How much of your family or national history do you know? Upon returning with the elders to Gilead, Jephthah sent messages to the king of Ammon asking why he was attacking Gilead. Jephthah also reminded the king of Ammon of their history and right to the land in dispute *(Judges 11:12–28)*. His living in Tob did not mean he lacked a full awareness of Israel's history. Brother, how much of your national history do you know or are you aware of? It doesn't really matter whether you now reside in your native homeland now or not.

How much of your family and national history are you teaching or passing on to your children? God created you to come from that family and that part of the world and there should be no shame or apologies about that.

Make peace not war

It would appear to me that Jephthah did not really want to engage in a physical battle if it could be avoided and so set up the dialogue channel which later failed. It's very rare to have a bloodless war or battle especially in this day and time, so please brother before you commit your people or troops to war utilise all that the Lord has made available to you.

When it became obvious that a war with the people of Ammon was inevitable, the Lord allowed His spirit to come upon Jephthah mightily *(verse 29).* Life is a battle, it's a war and without the presence of the Lord, in the person of the Holy Spirit, success cannot be guaranteed. If you will call upon the Lord, He will show up and anoint you for the task for which He has made you in Jesus' name. (Amen).

When you vow, always count the cost

On his way to fight, Jephthah made a costly vow to the Lord. That of sacrificing as a burnt offering whatever comes out of his home first upon God helping him to win the battle. Brother, you need to be careful on making vows to people and to God. No careless words please.

Indeed, Jephthah won the battle destroying all of Israel's enemies including the people from twenty cities. Only in the anointing of God can an ordinary man like Jephthah or yourself perform an extraordinary act like this! As he was returning from the same war, coming out of his own home was his only child who innocently was unaware of her father's vow welcoming him with timbrels and dances.:

'And it came to pass, when he saw her, that he rent his clothes, and said, Alas, my daughter! Thou hast brought me very low, and thou art one of them that trouble me: for I have opened my mouth unto the Lord, and I cannot go back.

His daughter agreed to her father's vow but asked that she be allowed to go with her friends and mourn her virginity for two months. 'And she said unto him, My father, if thou hast opened thy mouth unto the Lord, do to me according to that which hath proceeded out of thy mouth; forasmuch as the Lord hath taken vengeance for thee of thine enemies, even of the children of Ammon. And she said unto her father, Let this thing be done for me: let me alone two months, that I may go up and down upon the mountains, and bewail my virginity, I and my fellows'. Whether Jephthah actually killed his daughter as a burnt offering or prevented her from getting married, the fact remains that by his vow, he terminated the dreams, heart desires and life of his daughter.

Jephthah was sorry for making the wrong vow to the Lord and he allowed his daughter her last wish *(verses 36–39)*. After his daughter returned, Jephthah fulfilled his costly vow to the Lord. He was indeed a man of his words and integrity *(verse 39; Psalms 15:4b)*.

Jephthah made a vow to the Lord without counting the cost of his promise *(verses 30 and 31)* and with his promise he brought an untimely death to his daughter *(only child)* by making the wrong vow to the Lord *(verses 39 –40)*. His vow also meant he ended his own lineage for he neither had another child nor did he have the privilege of becoming a grandfather. Brother, what vows have you made to the Lord? In what ways have you endangered or terminated the lives of your children/ family with your vow to man or God? Was the vow worth it? Please take utmost care counting the cost before making a vow to God especially when it has to do with other members of your family who are not you.

In some professions, a vow is made or oath is sworn to become a full-fledged member. Part of the promise made during their swearing in, at least in some countries actually makes the newly qualified one swear to have their children do the same profession as the parent being sworn in. There have been many children from such families getting upset and unwilling to follow their parent's profession. This, many times, has cost the individual refusing to study that profession a lot of grief and sometimes lots of many years living unfulfilled and rebellious life.

The Bible did not say that Jephthah consulted his family nor informed them of his vow to the Lord at the time of the vow, yet instead of blaming himself for his grievous mistake, he accused his daughter of being among those who caused him grief! *'And it came to pass, when he saw her, that he rent his clothes, and said, Alas, my daughter! Thou hast brought me very low, and thou art one of them that trouble me: for I have opened my mouth unto the Lord, and I cannot go back' (verse 35)*. Please do not be like Jephthah, accept it when you are wrong and be humble to apologise. In other words, be willing and glad to eat the humble pie.

May we pray please?

> *Dear Father, thank You that I am not an accident that happened but a person whom You knew before conception, monitored in pregnancy, allowed to be born into the (name your family name).family. Father, thank You for accepting me and loving me just as I am. Thank You for my past which you are capable of using for my good and the benefit of those around me.*
>
> *Father, I present to You the following people or situations that have driven me away from my*

rightful inheritance. Father I ask in Jesus name, that all that the enemy has used against me to date be used from now for my good in Jesus name according to Romans 8:28.

Thank You Lord for the particular mission that You have for me in this life. Please help me to identify this mission and in Your love, mercy and favour, pour on me Your anointing through the Holy Spirit that in You and through You, I, an ordinary person may attain extraordinary achievements for You, in Jesus' name.

Father, I humbly bow before you, confessing the times I have made vows to men or to You Lord without counting the cost to my family (you may wish to list such occasions). I am sorry Lord and I ask for Your forgiveness. I ask for Your mercy at the times when I had mortgaged the future of my children for my own selfish reasons and personal ambition. Father, please show me Your mercy and deliver my family from untimely death, unprofitable ventures, setbacks and disillusionment in Jesus' name I pray with thanksgiving. Amen

Chapter 8

THE FATHER WHO DID NOT KNOW HIS CHILD.

Know your children

Jesse was the son of Obed, who was the son of Boaz and Ruth *(Ruth 4:17)*. Jesse had eight sons including David. No one knows if David shared the same mother with his seven elder brothers. Could it be that David was probably a result of a one-night stand affair child *(Psalms 51:5)?* David was the last boy in the family.

Jesse's first and second sons were in Saul's army but the Bible does not record where the third to the seventh sons were. We do know from the Bible that David, the eighth son, was alone with the sheep in the wilderness. Though Jesse had many sons, he seemed not to know David in particular. The Bible does not tell us why Jesse felt of all of his sons, David, the last boy, was to be sent to look after the family sheep alone in the wilderness. If David was illegitimate, his dad may have sent him away to conceal his shame and guilt or it may equally be that the practice then was for the younger one to look after the sheep. Jesse's lack of knowledge of who David was, was probably another reason why he failed to include him among his sons when Samuel asked him to present his sons before the Lord or he might have felt it would mean keeping the prophet waiting for long.

Father, how much do you know about your children, their likes or dislikes, what makes them happy or sad, what is their goal for life when they are of age, what hidden skills are in your children that are waiting to be recognised, nourished and used according to the word of God.

Treat your children right

Parents, be careful how you treat each child in the family. Children have eyes to see, ears to hear what is being said and feelings to know whether they are or are not loved by you. It is not unusual that the child you had the least hope for whatever reason will turn out at last to be the most honoured achiever and helper in your old age. Take time today father and begin to get to know your child. Many children are happier outside their family home. They will rather spend time with friends than their family especially if they feel unwanted, unloved, unappreciated or physically or emotionally bullied. Some children, unfortunately, are sexually harassed by members of their family, sometimes including their fathers. Father, the Bible warns you not to provoke your children to anger *(Ephesians 6:4 and Colosians 3:21).*

Be careful Dad how you treat each child and how you relate with each child. What you say or don't say; what you give or don't give; what you permit or don't permit with each child. As much as it is possible and practicable, be fair with each child accommodating their weaknesses and encouraging him or her in the area of strength.

As a father, your words to each child can be a blessing or a curse for in your tongue lies the power of life and death. Even in their failures, be particularly mindful of your utterances especially when you are upset.

Prophet Samuel's unannounced visit must have shocked Jesse. When asked to present his sons to the Lord, Jesse obeyed Samuel the prophet partially when he was asked to sanctify and present his sons. Knowingly or otherwise, he initially failed to send for David until the prophet specifically asked him to do so.

Jesse allowed two of his sons to fight in King Saul's army but he kept himself informed of their well being and encouraged them by sending David to visit them with some fruits and food and some for the war commanders too. Life in many ways is like a battle field, though your children may be old and may now be away from home, they sometimes would need your encouragements and support so please keep in touch with them. Good news from afar, the Bible says is like cold water to the thirsty *(Proverbs 25:25).*

At some point after the war against Goliath, King Saul sent to Jesse for him to release David to come and serve him. Jesse did not hesitate to send David to King Saul *(1 Samuel 16: 6–11).*

Accept your responsibility

Every father should realise that no child begged to come to the earth through any father's loins. Many men have pressurised their wives, mistresses or concubines to terminate pregnancies for social reasons, not because there was any serious medical sickness in the unborn child but because the man just wanted to protect his own identity and did not want to take the fatherly responsibility in the life of the unborn child. You may think the circumstances of that child's conception or birth is not right or ideal, the timing is wrong in your calendar of events, etc. Brother/father whatever makes you make love to that woman should make you take full responsibility to properly father the child. In God's calendar there is nothing like an accidental conception or birth for the Good Lord knew about it and allowed the pregnancy *(Genesis 38:1–26).* You owe God, yourself, your wife and that unborn or already born child a duty to love, cherish and protect their lives irrespective of the circumstances surrounding the conception or birth. Any grudge or disagreement that occurs between you the father and the mother should not adversely affect your relationship and love with that child neither should any disability especially congenital disability that the child may have make you love that child less.

Approve your children

Every child wants and seeks the approval and affirmation of their father and mother. It is bad enough for the father not to defend his child when looked down upon by others but it is very disturbing, worrisome and devastating when the father looks down or underestimates his child in anything. Because our views are limited, many fathers have underestimated their children who though started poorly but turned out to be the best and outstanding and helpful among all their children.

On the other hand, a number of matured adults are not doing well because their parents might have rejected or underestimated them becoming somebody important or productive in life. They may now be parents themselves, but are still living in the shadow of this rejection or underestimation. Brother, you owe no one the obligation to prove yourself; God knows all about you and loves you just as you are. Rather brother, should you find yourself in this situation; you would need talking and praying it through with a matured Christian or counsellor. Father/brother I appeal to you in the name of the Lord never to put down any of your children

Jesse exposed David to many dangers as a boy by sending him alone to tend the sheep and to take messages to his big brothers at war. Father, in what ways are you exposing your children to unnecessary dangers e.g. by your smoking, drinking, gambling, telling lies, stealing, etc. What risks are you taking by the things you ask them to do or not do, or by your attitude and why?

Perhaps you would like to say a prayer for yourself now as you compare your life with Jesse especially as it relates to your relationship with one or more of your children. You may wish to say a prayer like this:

> *Father, I come to You knowing full well that there is hope for me if only I could call on Your name. Thank you Lord for the children You have blessed me with. Thank You Lord that my quivers are full of them. Thank You Lord for the conception of each child including those conceived through me out of wedlock. Thank You Lord that you have good plans and thoughts towards each one of my seeds. Lord, I confess my wrong dealings with (insert name of child or children) and I apologise for my behaviour towards this child or these children. I ask for Your forgiveness, mercy and help that I need in dealing with my family especially this named child or children. I need Your love, compassion and grace to be all the good that I could be to my children in Jesus' name I pray with thanksgiving. Amen.*

Try within your means to be reconciled with any of your children or spouse or family whom you have hurt in times past.

Chapter 9

THE FATHER WHO OVER EXPOSED HIS CHILDREN.

Genesis 12:1-5, 13, 18-19-End

Lot followed his uncle Abraham out of the land of Hur and went with him everywhere until there were quarrels between his men and the men of Abraham his uncle with regards to insufficient food provision for their cattle. Lot probably was aware of the quarrels but did not seem to do anything positive to resolve it. Abraham called him and suggested a separation of the two families because of the fights. Lot did not object to the suggestion and agreed. Though younger, he agreed to choose first and he never prayed before making his choice.

Entertaining Angels unawares

Lot had many godly traits though he lived among an ungodly set of people. Whilst he could not influence the people in Sodom, he maintained his godliness. You don't have to join the group of bad people if you cannot positively influence in them for a better change.

Lot was very much welcoming to strangers *(Genesis 19:1-3).* He persuaded them to come under his roof for protection against the evils of the night. Little did Lot know about the three strangers. He volunteered to feed and entertain these strangers when he did not know who they were. He fed them with the best of his animals and food. Lot tried to save the lives of these guests from the wicked gay men *(Genesis 19:4-7).* There are many out there on the streets, strangers perhaps in your community unaware of the dangers who you may need to invite to your home or and church primarily for their protection and feeding and secondarily for their salvation. Lot used his resources to fend for these strangers so should you and I.

Seeking God's divine choices

Lot's choice of land was by sight not by the leading of the Holy Spirit - one which he later would regret. He moved his family to and settled in Sodom. Lot could have moved away from Sodom, yet for reasons known to him alone he chose to stay among the wicked. *"Blessed is the man that walketh not in the counsel of the ungodly, nor standeth in the way of sinners, nor sitteth in the seat of the scornful." (Psalms 1:1).* Brother, where have you moved your family to live in? Could it be that Lot was trying to save his face by remaining amongst the wicked when he could have relocated to another place once he found out that the Sodomites were up to nothing?

Lot upon hearing the impending danger warned his sons-in-laws but they did not heed him *(Genesis 19:14).* There was no time to pack any of his belongings, but Lot obeyed the angels and left Sodom with his immediate family *(Genesis 19:15–16).* Father, there are times that you might have to move your family to safety without much warnings, heeding to godly instructions could be the only way to save your family from the oncoming danger. Remember Joseph had to move Mary and Baby Jesus urgently to Egypt until the reigning king died.

During the 1966 Nigerian Civil War, my family was caught up in Port Harcourt, in the eastern part of Nigeria. Days into the war, as I was told later, my mum had been saying to my dad that we should return to our family base in the south west. Dad felt the rioting would soon stop and there would be no need for us to travel but at the last minute, there was a radio announcement advising non-Easterners to leave for their own safety. My dad did not waste time in getting our family out in a matter of hours. We left our newly equipped flat with so little if anything. We were among the last most fortunate people to cross the Onitsha bridge before it was bombed! It was an experience I cannot forget.

As a father, are you greedy when the opportunity to choose comes or do you seek God's face only before you choose? The things that are not seen many times are more real than those that are seen, choosing by sight only without consulting God often leads to problems, complications and death if care is not taken. Lot moved to Sodom and lived in the wrong community of men who did not know or fear God. Though he managed to keep his faith yet he was not able to positively affect the community in which he found himself. He was not a good influence on the men who worked for him either unlike Abraham. The reason we know this is that his herdsmen fought with Abraham's men over the land *(Genesis 13:5–8)* and when God agreed to save Sodom on account of ten people *(Genesis 18:31–32),* ten people could not be found even in his family including his potential sons-in-law or servants!

Nowhere in the scriptures was it mentioned that Lot raised an altar unto the Lord, not even after he and his family had been rescued from the complete annihilation of Sodom. One who is not grateful and thankful to God for His blessing will not be grateful to human beings. He missed out on a covenant blessing and relationship with God.

Sold out to whom?

Lot was willing to give his virgin daughters to strangers to abuse (*Genesis 19:4-8).* At what price was Lot willing to protect his visitors? Father, how protective are you of those in your care especially those innocent children given to you by God to tend and bring up? Are you one of those fathers who abuse your children emotionally, physically or sexually or in your desperation, do you turn these innocent ones over to the wicked to do to as is good in their eyes? Or perhaps you have signed your children and their generations to come unknowingly to the wicked one. Have you deliberately drawn your children into the occult or indebtedness, verbal, physical, emotional or sexual abuse in pursuit of your ambitions or at the time of your challenges?

Who among your children or family members or vulnerable, innocent ones that you have picked from the street pretending to want to help have you maimed or killed to achieve your wealth or position or satisfy your ungodly passion brother? I'll like to remind you of the wordings of the song *'You cannot hide it from God, you may cover your sins so that no one may know you cannot hide it from God'.*

It is not too late to repent father and call on the Lord, for God is able to redeem these innocent ones that you have freely given to the wicked to do to as 'good' in their eyes. Have you sold any of your children, siblings or relatives for money or into the sex or drug trade?

This is a call for the leaders of every nation. Into which bondage, yoke, borrowing deals like the IMF loan have you signed your nation into whilst you keep acquiring and amazing wealth abroad? This is a call too to Church leaders, pastors and vicars. How many innocent children have you abused or are abusing? 'A vicar has been jailed for three-and-a-half years for amassing a collection of more than 56,000 indecent images of children. The Reverend Richard Hart, 59, of Whopshott Avenue, Horsell, Woking, appeared before Cardiff Crown Court after pleading guilty at an earlier hearing to 12 charges of making indecent images of children, four of taking indecent photographs of children and five of possessing such images in offences dating back as far as 1991'

From AOL website homepage of 25/9/08

Abuser or the abused?

Are you one of those fathers who unashamedly abuse their children or other people's children left in your care out of trust? How do you see your child? Like a sex toy to be abused or a child to be cherished, cared for and nourished? You may get away from the law of the land but you will not escape God's wrath or judgement. You should know that. God is and will forgive you if you repent of your wickedness and return no more to your sins. You need to come open and clean of this evil to your pastor, matured Christian or counsellor and seek counsel. You will need to seek for the forgiveness not only of God but of all the ones whose lives you have messed up.

Many are not able to keep a relationship or marriage today because of their childhood abuse. They had sustained wounds unutterably inflicted upon their innocent heart by heartless and wicked family members or associates. If you find yourself being the victim and are struggling, there is hope too for you in Jesus' name and blood. You too need to come open to your pastor, matured Christian or counsellor and seek counsel. You may need help primarily from God and support of your pastor, matured Christian or counsellor in coming to terms with forgiving those who have messed up your life and learn to begin to experience a clean life in Jesus' name.

Lot was able not to look back on his possession as commanded by the angels as they were fleeing for their safety. There is the saying that once there is still life there is hope. There may be need to cut off yourself practically from every earthly possession, position or project and focus on God and where He is leading you to. Whatever you are willing to walk away from as God speaks to you, will determine what you are likely going to receive later. Abraham walked away from Hur and he was blessed with the land of Canaan. Joseph was forced out of his home but he later became the Prime Minister in Egypt. Moses ran from becoming the Pharaoh in Egypt and God ordained him, used him to lead up to three million Israelites out of the land of Egypt. The little boy gave Jesus his five loaves of bread and some fishes and there were twelve basketfuls left over when all had eaten.

Lot had good negotiating spirit or interceding attitude for he was able to negotiate with the angels to a nearby destination *(Genesis 19:17–20).* Father, how good are you at interceding for others or in negotiating?

Find where you belong and settle for no less.

Instead of trusting God to get him the mountains, Lot settled for the nearby little city *(Genesis 19:4-7)* and ended up living in a cave out of fear *(Genesis 19:30).* Father/brother in which ways have you settled for the convenient, not necessarily God's own desire for you? Have you then had to live in fear in the choice you made? Where are you living or hiding now because of fear? Why continue to be tormented by the spirit of fear when the Bible says God has not given us the spirit of fear but of love, power and sound mind - *2 Timothy 1:7.* God is the God of second chance if you will in humility seek His face in repentance, He is able to restore you. Stop settling for the good and manageable. Go for the best, at least you are a child of the Most High God.

Creating effective communication channels

Having to flee for their life was bad but the Bible did not say Lot took time later to speak to:

a God who saved him and his family and gave him another chance of beginning again in a new place. God who brought him and his family out of destruction sure had another plan for their lives but the Bible did not say that Lot took time to seek the face of the Lord for this. What a missed opportunity and future.

b Abraham his uncle for any form of support or advice. It would seem that Lot did not maintain family ties with Abraham or contacted him after this event. There is a place for friends and family especially in times of catastrophe or joy.

Everyone has his or her place. Don't neglect your friends

or family for you never can tell when you will need their support. Perhaps if he had contacted his uncle, Abraham would have sent him some goods, etc, to set him up again and perhaps suitable suitors for his daughters or advised him on how to get his daughters properly married.

c his daughters about the possibility of their marriage in the new environment since their suitors had perished in the brimstone and fire at Sodom and Gomorrah. The Bible did not tell us that Lot had a family or counselling session with any of his virgin daughters especially then that their mother had turned into a pillar of salt and with the destruction of their home and potential spouses. It might be that he was pre-occupied with his loss or on how to begin again after escaping from Sodom. Many fathers for whatever reasons leave the sexual education/training of their children to their friends, school, Internet, soaps, and ungodly magazine that show sexual lust and sexual gratification outside the context of the godly marriage. Ungodly sexual counselling always goes against God and His laws, which He has given to mankind for mankind's protection. It is natural at certain age to want to have intimacy with the opposite sex but if these emotions are not properly channelled or addressed, it might bring unhappiness to all concerned in the long run. Lot probably forgot that his daughters:

- ❖ Were of age.
- ❖ Were in their prime time with the possibility of wanting to be sexually active.

- ❖ Were living in a godless society.
- ❖ Had been exposed to a society filled with immoral sexual actions.

As a father, what preparations are you making for your daughter's/son's wedding? When should you start making preparations towards it too? What preparations are necessary for your children's wedding? Is there any need for a father to plan and prepare for his child's wedding?

Fathers who don't spend quality time dating their children, talking to them about their life's goals, aspirations and marriage should not complain about who their daughter marry or their son impregnates.

There are at least four great influences on the children today apart from their parents/family and teachers. They are namely the literature they read, the friends and company they keep, the music they listen to and the television/movie programmes that they watch. How well, father, are you familiar with your children's taste in these areas?

**'There are six things that you owe your children:

- ❖ **Instruct them** – *Deuteronomy 6: 6 –7*
- ❖ **Train them** – *Proverbs 22: 6*
- ❖ **Provide for them** – *2 Corinthians 12 :14*
- ❖ **Nurture them** – *Ephesians 6: 4*
- ❖ **Discipline them** – *1 Timothy 3:4, Proverbs*
- ❖ **Love them** – *Titus 2: 4.*

Lot did some things wrong: things that ultimately cost him his family:

- ❖ He had the wrong emphasis – he placed financial success above spiritual priorities.
- ❖ He lived in the wrong environment – he thought his children could live in Sodom and not be affected by it.
- ❖ He had the wrong expectations – he thought he could change Sodom by compromising with it.
- ❖ He had the wrong example – he thought his children would follow instructions but instead they followed his lifestyle.
- ❖ He had the wrong relationships – he didn't realise until it was too late how much Sodom had influenced his family. *Genesis 19: 1-38***

**'From the Word for Today by Bob and Debby Gass with Ruth Gass Halliday July 25 2003.'

You can't live by the rules of the world and think your child or children will follow God's rules. Have you ever noticed that little children love to wear their Mum's or Dad's big shoes and wondered why? As you walk in God's truth they are most likely going to follow in your footsteps.

Perhaps you would like to say a prayer for yourself now that you have compared your life with Lot. May we pray together please?

Father, You alone know me more than I know myself. Thank You Father for showing me the following areas where I could have done better (you may wish to list them). I am grateful that I can come to You confessing my sins and asking not only for Your forgiveness and cleansing but also for Your Grace to live positively for You from now on.

Lord, I realize that out of greed, I have made some wrong choices (you may wish to list them) and now I have moved into the camp of the ungodly, I find myself not being a positive influence on these ungodly people, I have and am exposing my family to ungodly living in its fullness daily. Father, please I need Your help in getting back to my roots in You even if that means losing all that I have greedily acquired, moving away to another place, changing jobs, friends and associates. Father, please help me to be willing to do all that You will ask me to do in getting back to You together with my household in Jesus' name I pray.

Lord, I need Your help in maintaining my family and friends ties, in becoming more welcoming and loving to strangers and those I can help, in taking time to talk and pray with my children with regards to their marriage and future. Thank You Lord for Your abiding presence and guidance and please help me to be obedient to You in all things in Jesus' name I pray with thanksgiving (Amen).

**For fathers who in times past have abused any children please say this prayer meaning every word of your prayers:

> *Dear Lord, I come in the name of Jesus Christ Your son, ashamed of my attitude and acts that made me abuse this child/these children (please name them) physically, emotionally, spiritually and sexually. I have no excuse or justification for all these wicked, shameful, heartless and godless acts of mine. Now that I know much better, Lord indeed I cannot quantify the hurt – physical, emotional or sexual distress I have caused the above named child/ren. I come just as I am with no plea. Lord, I approach You in the name of Jesus asking for Your forgiveness and total cleansing according to Isaiah 1:18, 30:15 and 1 John 1:8-9. Lord, as I prayerfully seek forgiveness from these precious ones whom I have hurt, I ask that I may not try to justify my sinful acts or cause more hurt but that I may receive their forgiveness too and from now live a clean and purposeful life in Jesus' name I pray.*

Brother, you surely need to come open and clean of this evil to your pastor or matured Christian/counsellor and seek counsel.

*** Please say meaningfully this prayer with me should you have been the victim of childhood or adulthood abuse be it physical, emotional, spiritual or sexual.

Dear Father, You alone knows the physical, emotional, spiritual and/or sexual abuse I have been subjected to so far in my life, wounds too deep for me to clean, invisible emotional scars or sores which cannot be seen even by the best of today's technology, hurts too deep for me to share with anyone but You. Who will believe my story but You alone who saw and know it all. For so long, I have pretended as if all was normal but deep down in me I know I am hurting, sad, I feel dirty, confused sometimes, lonely, depressed, withdrawn from other people who perhaps could have been able to help me, often I cannot make sense of what life is all about anyway, (please feel free to confess how you truly feel to God your Father). Lord I come to You today for only in You can I find my life, peace, joy, innocence, myself, hope and health again. Lord please forgive me of my sins, cleanse me with Your blood and make me whole again, body soul and spirit in Jesus name. Lord it is humanly impossible to freely forgive those who have abused and oppressed me so far but in Your mercies and grace, I need Your help in not only coming to terms with my past which I no longer have control over but trusting only in You Lord, with Your help, I choose to forgive those who abused me (you may wish to mention names here) because You have forgiven me too in Jesus' name. Amen

Lord, I struggle in the following areas of my life as a result of the abuse (mention them) and I give them to you from now in Jesus name. Please Lord, help me rebuild my shattered life and make it beautiful, fruitful and purposeful again I pray in Jesus name and with thanksgiving. Amen.

You too need to come open and tell of this evil to your pastor or matured Christian counsellor and seek counsel.

Please read this song prayerfully and allow the Holy Spirit to heal you through it:

OH LORD YOUR TENDERNESS

O Lord, Your tenderness
Melting all my bitterness
O Lord I receive Your love. [2]
O Lord, Your loveliness
Changing all my ugliness
O Lord I receive Your love.
O Lord I receive Your love.

Source: http://www.turnbacktogod.com/oh-lord-your-tenderness-song

USEFUL CONTACTS:

Full Gospel Business Men's International Fellowship:
http://www.fgbmfi.org/
+1 949 461 0100

SOME SEXUAL ABUSE HELP LINES IN THE UK:

Off Record

Tel. Number 0208 251 0251

Face to face

Tel. Number 0208 667 0207

Rape & Sexual Abuse Support

Tel. Number 0208 683 3311

OTHERS:

The Shepherd's Ministries
5 Brookehowse Road
Bellingham
London SE6 3TJ, UK
Tel/Fax: +44 208 698 7222
Email: info@theshepherdsministries.org
Website: www.theshepherdsministries.org

Your local Social Services help line should be able to direct you appropriately.

IN NIGERIA:

Children's Evangelism Ministry Inc
P.O. Box 4480
Ilorin, Kwara State,
Nigeria.
Tel: +234 31 222199
E-mail: cem@ilorin.skannet.com

Teenagers' Outreach Ministries
www.teenagersoutreachministries.Org.

IN USA:

www.eCounseling.com
Tel Number: 1-866-268-6735
Make a contact today if you or someone you know needs help. You are only one phone call away from help for all forms of abuse including sexual abuse.

Chapter 10

THE DRUNKEN FATHER.

Genesis Chapters 6 – 9

A useful vessel

Lamech named his son Noah for he said '*this same shall comfort us concerning our work and toil of our hands, because of the ground which the Lord hath cursed' (Genesis 5:29).* By the time of his birth, Noah's father felt there was need for comfort from the human toil and work. Brother, what was the expectation of your parents when they gave you that name? How have you been able to fulfil that expectation?

At the time Noah lived, there was so much evil that the Lord could not but destroy the whole world He had made. However, Noah was found faithful to God and righteous such that God decided to spare his life and that of his immediate family. Nothing could be farther from the truth in the saying 'if you can't beat them, join them'. We need to realize that each one born of a woman will stand one day before the righteous God to be judged. Man may not acknowledge your godly living but

God certainly sees it all, and He is so faithful that in the midst of destruction He will save the godly ones.

Without holiness no man can see God, says the Bible. God is still looking for men who though are in the world are not of the world, men who will live godly lives in an ungodly world; clean vessels who have a relationship with Him and are available for His plans and purposes alone. God will always forgive the sinner but after forgiveness there is need to live in line with His Words and ways if you are to be used by Him.

Noah had a relationship with God and was able to hear God's instruction for safety from the impending world calamity. Noah was able to hear and take down the details of the architectural design of the ark - a project that had not been done before. Noah must have consulted God many times in the course of the project. Brother/father, how will you describe your relationship with God in recent times and can you say you have heard from Him recently, even today? In that God given project or assignment, brother, when last did you consult Him who sent you?

Noah obeyed God totally in completing the ark and filling it with all kinds of all the animals, birds and he had enough food for them. It was a project that took many years to complete on dry land and at a time when it had not rained and the world was under the green house effect. Many scholars say it took 120 years to construct the ark by Noah and his family, far from the rivers or seas, one which had not been done before.

Can you imagine if Noah did not hear or obey God when He was called? This was a project that demanded all of his time, knowledge, skills, endurance, patience and resources and he did not compromise on any of the details he had been shown by God. My guess is that many came round to mock or ridicule him while obeying God in constructing this ark as God instructed.

Some qualities of a pioneer

To be the first in anything especially in that which the Lord has called you to be or laid upon your heart to do will demand of you the good qualities in Noah's life. Are you prepared for that or will you rather compromise or join the crowd? Or perhaps you think the world is too big for God to notice you and your actions good or bad, may I remind you that he knows you so much in details to the hair on your head, the words you have not yet formed in your mind and your address. *See Psalms 139:13–16, Acts 10:1-6, Isaiah, Jeremiah 1:5.*

Noah was a multi- skilled, multi- talented man, he was an ark maker, an engineer, a zoologist, a weather forecast man, a vineyard farmer, a wine maker just to name a few. Brother, do you know you are a multi-skilled, multi-talented man and that all that you need to fulfil your destiny is already in you? You may need to listen to those around you and watch your desires and actions in finding out more of your God given skills and talents. As you find them, please use them appropriately to the

Glory of your maker and the blessing of the people around you.

A God-given project

Noah was capable of commanding the support of his children, in-laws and many others during this long-term project. In that God given assignment or project brother, how able are you to command the support of others? Learn to build relationships not transactions.

I believe God created and chose Noah for the purposes of continuity of mankind. Noah's destiny was locked in hearing God, obeying God, building the ark and preserving pairs each of God's creation (animals, reptiles and birds). Whatever he was doing before the revelation of building the ark had to be left. Beloved have you found your assignment in this world yet? Do you know your destiny in Christ yet? Are you pursuing the calling of the Lord for your life or you are still doing your thing and in your way?

After Noah completed the building of the ark and getting in all the animals, reptiles, birds and his family into the ark, it took a few days of waiting before God Himself closed the door of the ark and the rains started falling. When you have done all that needs to be done in your God given errand or assignment, you need to be still and have faith in God for Him to come and confirm or bless your work. God will surely show up brother so don't give in to the enemy nor give up on God.

The same rain that killed every living creation at the flood was used by God to protect Noah and his family transporting them higher unto safety, success and victory. My prayer for you is that the same thing that has made many to fall will be used by God to make you to stand tall, strong, catapulted and promoted above your enemies in Jesus' name. The devil might have made plans and meant it for evil, God will turn it around for your provision, protection and blessings in Jesus' name. Amen.

And the Lord remembers

The rain fell for forty days and forty nights with Noah, his family and his zoo boxed in for one hundred and fifty more days afterwards *(Genesis 7:24–8:14).* Then the Lord remembered Noah; the water dried up and God brought their ark to safe landing and they were all let go to make a living for themselves. The story usually changes for good and breakthrough when the Lord remembers anyone. The Lord remembered Hannah, the Israelites, Noah, may He remember you too in Jesus name.

Whatever has boxed you in the name of Jesus cannot but spew you out and let you go in Jesus name, in order for you to be released into God's blessing and destiny. May the Lord remember you and your household for victory in every area of your lives in Jesus' name.

Building an altar of praise

After coming out alive from the ark, the Bible records that Noah did build an altar to God. The Bible is silent on how Noah and his family felt while it rained. Certainly, their experience would have been more than a few weeks ship travel. Coming out of the ark to dry land truly needed a thanksgiving to the Lord. Brother how many times has God protected you or your loved ones from a glaring death or destruction or unpleasant uncertainties of life? You and I need to give Him praise and build an altar of thanksgiving to Him because if not for God where would you and I be today *(Psalms 124:1-8)?*

The rainbow, God's promise

It was after Noah sacrificed unto the Lord, that God made him and mankind a covenant of not destroying the world again with water and He left us the rainbow as a sign in the sky for mankind to always remember. Your sacrificial giving cannot but attract God's mercy, covenant of peace and protection. Whenever and wherever you see the rainbow, remember God's promises and His faithfulness to keep His promises. It ought to be an opportunity to use the rainbow to teach your children about God's faithfulness in spite of our sins.

Missing the mark

Noah later planted a vineyard and from its fruits he made some wine. He drank the wine and got drunk! In his drunken status, he lay naked in his tent. When he woke up, he never acknowledged nor confessed his sins, let alone repent of his drunkenness to his family rather he cursed one of his children's offspring. The same Noah whom God found righteous now a drunkard! How do you explain that? Simply, in us all, even the very best of the best lies the potential of falling short of God's glory and standard *(Romans 3:23).* The fact that you are successful today does not preclude you from falling tomorrow unless you continuously abide in His will. The Bible also says let him who thinks he stands be careful lest he falls.

There is too much stress and lots of challenges in the world today. Father, if you cannot bless your family like David did in *2 Samuel 20:6* then, for God's sake don't curse them either. The price of living under any curse cannot be quantified especially when the curse is from a parent. *See 2 Chronicles 4:9-10.*

Watch what you say father, when your secret has been let out, when your weakness has been exposed, when the truth about any matter has been exposed.

There is no perfect father, every child gets to know that with time, but children and wives usually want a father who, when he has made a mistake, rather than pretend or sweep it under the carpet, will openly acknowledge his mistake, confess his sins before God, repenting of his sins, and openly acknowledging his mistakes to his children and family. Noah ought to have apologised to his sons for being drunk and for exposing himself in his drunkenness. He should have used the opportunity to address his weakness and the effects of drunkenness rather he covered up by cursing one of his son's generations yet unborn.

Yours might not be drunkenness like Noah but pornography or sexual, physical, psychological or emotional abuse of wife or children or house help or relatives or colleagues. It may be cheating, intense anger, unforgiveness, lying, murmuring, constant complaining, quarrelling, drugs or wife-beating, extra marital affairs, stealing or armed robbery, negative gang activities, and occult practices to name a few. Own up to your sins; don't think your children don't see or know, however young they are. Don't curse them to shut them up, own up and ask for forgiveness from God and the people involved. Turn your sin into another opportunity to teach and train your children the effects of such sins *(Psalms 51),* David promised to teach transgressors the way of the Lord once his relationship was once again right with God.

Cover the nakedness

Should you as a child find any aspect of your father's life uncovered in a shameful way, then I suggest:

- ❖ You cover that nakedness as much as you could and discretely.
- ❖ Pray against same issue happening to you now or later and prayerfully map out things that you may need to do to avoid such occurrence in your own life.
- ❖ Acknowledge the fact that there is need to seek the face of the Lord for victory. You might need to intercede for your dad and your family.
- ❖ When your father is sober, in the right atmosphere and mood seek an audience with him on one to one on how he may be helped. You may need to support him seek for counselling from one of the fore mentioned organizations.
- ❖ Avoid taunting your father with his weakness.

Do you mind if we pray together before you continue reading the book please?

Dear Lord Jesus, thank You for making me in Your image for Your Glory and Honour. Thank You Lord, that I have been created and chosen for a purpose. Help me Lord to live a life that can hear from You about my God-assigned destiny and fulfil it in Jesus' name. Give me Lord, a clear mind, an understanding and obedient heart to follow You. Give me Lord all the resources human beings inclusive, that is required for the starting and successful completion of my destiny.

Thank you, Lord, for sparing my life and that of my family and friends especially for the recent miracles of deliverance.

Father, please I need Your help in this area where I have been struggling and exposing my nakedness (drunkenness or you might wish to name them all). Father, I apologise for trying to cover my shortcomings and cursing of the following people unnecessarily (name them). I repent of this wrong and I apply the blood of Jesus to neutralise the curses in Jesus' name. From now help me Lord to daily pronounce Your blessings as written in Your word to those whom I have previously cursed in Jesus' name I pray with thanksgiving. Amen

If you would like to quit drinking or any other substance abuse please visit- www.christianrecoveryministries.com or http://www.aa-intergroup.org/urgent/index.php or

IN USA:

www.eCounseling.com
Tel Number: 1-866-268-6735
Make a contact today if you or someone you know needs help.

Chapter 11

THE ENVIOUS FATHER.

When loss launches into destiny

Saul, the son of Kish and a servant were asked by his father to go and look for some of their donkeys that had gone missing. After many days of search, Saul told the servant it was time for them to return home as the donkeys were not found and he felt his father by that time would then be concerned with their whereabouts rather than the missing donkeys. His servant advised that they consult Prophet Samuel 'the seer' who was nearby. As he had nothing to offer, the servant volunteered that which he had to give to the 'seer'. It is a wise idea to take some present/gift *(within your means)* and give to the prophet God has assigned to you in life. This is not necessarily because they are in lack but to appreciate God's gift in their lives.

It is not unusual that many run into their God-assigned destiny by mistake, by one form of loss or the other, which they have submitted unto God. Brother, what have you just lost that you are searching for? God has another plan if only you will spend quality time in His presence and perhaps seek godly counsel.

God does not require that you and I be somebody before we approach Him but to come just as we are, the price and sacrifice have been paid for by Jesus His son. Come today just as you are, in your loss, uncertainty, frustration, come brother, God is waiting for you. Jesus said 'come unto me all of you who are burdened and heavy laden and I will give you rest'.

A better and more rewarding plan

What Saul did not realise was that God had a better plan for him which was to be unveiled to him when he got to Prophet Samuel. He approached Samuel to ascertain the probability of finding the missing donkeys but he left with a realisation of what God had in future for him. It does not matter how and why you come to Christ, you are guaranteed He will meet that need and much more. Shout a big hallelujah as your destiny is about to take a new and better turn from now in Jesus' name. God who brought Saul from obscurity to become the number one person in Israel is able to move you from obscurity to popularity. Samuel anointed Saul for his task, told him the donkeys had been found, gave him details of what would happen as he left and told him what he should do in the circumstances.

With the anointing of God now upon Saul, he began to experience divine connections and favour – meeting men who were carrying bread and they gave him most of the loaves they were carrying, he became qualified to and joined in the company of the sons of the prophets and he experienced the presence of the Holy Spirit manifesting the gift of prophecy.

Don't lose your opportunities

Saul became king at the age of forty and ruled Israel for thirty two years. He had opportunities to succeed. Let's examine some points in his favour:-

- ❖ He was the first king of Israel - God's chosen person. God doesn't choose any person or leader without His full support, wisdom and direction which is available to the person for as long as he or she seeks the Lord.
- ❖ He was a much wanted king by the nation. The people were prepared to give him their support and loyalty in spite of the implications this may bring unto them *(1 Samuel 8:5-20)* especially *verses 19-20.*
- ❖ He had God's anointing oil twice and the Holy Spirit's anointing *(1 Samuel 10:1 and 10:6).* You might wish to compare this with Acts 1:8.
- ❖ He had good physical qualities - he was head and shoulder taller than everyone else in Israel *(1 Samuel 10:23).*
- ❖ He was a diplomatic man. Because he was forty years old when he became king he obviously had some experience and maturity behind him. When one of his uncles wanted to find out what Samuel had told him, Saul answered tactically without giving away God's message to him *(1 Samuel 10:15-16).*

- Samuel loved him and was there for him, Saul could have had the company and advice of one of the most favoured prophet of old *(1 Sam 15:11)*. Brother, God loves you and I, the sweet Holy Spirit is there for all believers today for direction, leadership and counselling.
- Saul refused to kill those who initially did not support him.

Sound the alarm if need be

King Saul and his men were at war with the Philistines and Goliath was threatening and disrespecting the God of Israel. He like his men was no physical match for the giant and in them was an obvious fear. King Saul then put up an advert for a rescuer of the embarrassing and prolonged situation. No one in the camp came forward but little David the shepherd boy. Brother, the fact that you cannot handle a situation does not mean no one else can. Learn to prayerfully put up an advert in the right places and your own person will one day show up.

When David was brought to King Saul, he told David 'you are not able to go against the Philistine to fight with him, for you are but a youth while he has been a warrior from his youth' *(1 Samuel 17:33)*. What King Saul like many today failed to realise is that:

- the battle is the Lord's and He decides whom He will use for the job.
- the anointing of God brings the victory not necessarily the age, weapons or the experience of the warriors.

- ❖ estimating what a person can or cannot do by their looks can be very wrong. God many times will choose to use the weak to shame the strong, the unlearned to shame the wise and learned, the poor to shame the rich. God is in the business of using ordinary people to achieve extraordinary acts. Such was Samson to the Philistines and at another time Gideon to their enemies.
- ❖ God will many times bring your solution in unattractive and unpopular vessels.

Equip your family and staff

King Saul, however, after listening to David's updated Curriculum Vitae (CV) *(1 Samuel 17:34-39)* consented to him fighting Goliath. He equally gave David his garments, bronze helmet and armour. Good as that might have been, Saul's fighting gear was unsuitable for David. Brother, how adequately have your equipped the people fighting your corner for you or better still how much protection are you giving to your staff (be it your driver, cleaner, personal assistant (PA), etc.) or family. Brother, to provide an unsuitable work/battle outfit is as dangerous as not providing one in the first instance. An unsuitable outfit gives your employees a false impression of protection. How many governments send their soldiers to war ill-equipped for the type of the enemy their soldiers will be contending with? For those in the business world, do you use child labour facilities? Do you deprive your staff of their rights and make them to work under threats, do you treat them as equals for they are human beings like yourself or do you threat them like animals? Do you pay their wages on time or you tend to owe them many months wages and then complain they are not giving you their best? Are you in any way abusing your staff physically, emotionally, sexually, financially or spiritually? Which is more important to you, your staff welfare and well being or your profits? Remember God made them like you, they are human beings to treasure not trashed, esteemed not abused especially when they are working for your interest. Have you considered including in their pay package things like health and life insurance schemes? May I remind you brother that the Lord harkens to the voice of the poor and expects that your employees are paid well and on time *(see Proverbs 22:16, 22-23, 16:8)*.

Beware of jealousy and its fruits

Following David's victory over Goliath, Jonathan, King Saul's son became friendly with David. They were possibly age mates and unknown to King Saul, Jonathan had made a covenant with David because he loved him as himself *(1 Samuel 18:1-4)*. This love is not homosexual love or relationship! King Saul was not particularly pleased at Jonathan's friendship with David.

David brought victory to God and Israel and life to King Saul and his men. However instead of thanking the Lord and finding security in God, he became unnecessarily jealous and insecure because the women were singing not just in his praise but also David's. He became deceitful and sought for ways of killing David. First, by luring him to marry one of his daughters *(1 Samuel 18:6-26)* at another time by sending for David to kill him, *(1 Samuel 19:9-17),* another time by using his spear to try to pin David into the wall (1 Samuel 19:9-10) and many more times King Saul and his troops pursued him into the wilderness to kill him.

Because of his spirit of jealousy, God took His anointing of peace from him and he became fearful and had a tormenting spirit. Brother, thank God and be contented with your own blessings. Being jealous of another child of God - your wife, child, friend etc inclusive will open you up to satanic oppression of many forms.

King Saul at another time attempted to kill his son Jonathan on account of David *(1 Samuel 20:1-34).* He was displeased at Jonathan's friendship with David. Before you criticise or condemn any of your children's friends, please spend some time knowing your child and that friend. Find out in particular why your child is fond of that friend. God has a plan for each child so don't think or conclude that a godly friend could jeopardise your child's position in life as King Saul did *(1 Samuel 20:32).* It is natural to be concerned with any ungodly associations that your child may have but you may be unable to separate them. What you could so in such a situation is for you to invite such an friend into your home on visits. Prayerfully spend time with this friend, get to know them better and perhaps why your child is so much attached, pray for the friend and your child and ask God for wisdom and godly love in such a challenging situation.

Avoidable failure:

Saul failed in the end and died untimely because:

- Saul disobeyed God when he went to war. God through Samuel instructed Saul to destroy everything, people, goods, cattle and so on because He wanted to punish the Amalekites. Saul destroyed only things that were despised and worthless. He and his men kept what they thought were the best of everything for themselves. Partial obedience is complete disobedience. Taking and keeping whatever God has not blessed nor ordained for you could be the beginning of your downfall and God's rejection *(1 Samuel 15:1-23).*
- Saul was not repentant of his earlier mistake *(1 Samuel 13:11-15).* When confronted by Samuel, Saul lied and tried covering up instead of confessing his sins to God and repenting, he tried justifying his ungodly action of disobedience, taking and keeping cursed items. One of the greatest differences between Saul and David in their rulership was that while both sinned and were confronted, Saul mostly tried to justify his sins whilst David confessed his, repented and sought for God's forgiveness and cleansing. Brother, are you always trying to justify your ungodly actions? Proverbs says you can justify your actions but God looks at our motives.

Is it not true that the society, the Church and perhaps some of those reading this book frown at some 'sins' and water down other sins as an acceptable norm e.g. premarital sex or relationship, homosexuality, and unforgiveness which can destroy spiritually and physically many times with physical manifestations ranging from aches and pains to possible incurable diseases.. To forgive may be difficult but it is not impossible. The sin of gossiping within the Church is yet another sin God frowns at *(Proverbs 6:16-19)*. Let us remember that whatever ideologies the society may put up, God's standards remains unchanging. He is not going to bend His rule to suit us. What God is against in the beginning, He will be against till Jesus comes back!

The cost of sin

Sin cuts us away from God. No matter how long you and I have been coming to church, being active, except we confess our sins individually and as a Church, we may be unable to hear God or experience God's move in our lives and in our midst. For instance the sin of Achan comes to mind. One man sinned but over thirty six people paid for it. Defeat was experienced by God's people in a seemingly successful battle. No one can deceive God.

Saul listened to the voice of man rather than the voice of God *(1 Samuel 13:6-11 and 1 Samuel 15:20-21)*. Any leader or leadership that seeks first the approval of man rather than

God is bound to fail and fall. God will never share His glory with any man. God will not compete for the rulership of any life, group or church, or with anything else. A careful search through the scriptures shows that people and leaders who put God first rather than man succeeded and vice versa e.g. Gideon, David, Joseph, Solomon etc.

God is never too late

Saul was an impatient person *(1 Samuel 13:8-10).* A little patience in waiting for Samuel for the sacrifice could have saved Saul from God's rejection. *'In quietness and trust shall be your strength', says Isaiah 30:15.* 'They that wait upon the Lord shall renew their strength' says Isaiah 40:31; they that put their trust in the Lord shall not be put to shame (Romans 10:4). Brother, I may not know your request and may not know for how long you have you been waiting for the fulfilment of your heart's desire, but don't give up or act irrationally instead of waiting on God. Don't place yourself in a position that is not meant for you as it can be very dangerous. When the demon of delay attacks and you are tempted to have and use your self-designed 'Plan B' remember that God's time and methods are not like ours, He is never too late or early. 'Though the vision tarries, it shall surely come to pass' *(Habakkuk 2:3).* Jumping God's gun has never paid any man - Abraham being a typical example.

Whose voice do you hear and obey? In the issues concerning your life or family, whose voice do you hear and obey? In the issues of your life, whose voice matters, God's or man's? Without faith it is impossible to please God *(Hebrews 11:6a).* God is not going to strive with any other voice. The Holy Spirit is available to teach, instruct and lead each one of us if we would avail ourselves of this wonderful opportunity.

Saul was the first God chosen and anointed king over Israel but he was not the high priest. The position of the king is distinct and different to the position of the high priest - both are valuable to God and mankind and both with separate job descriptions. Saul, due to impatience and the fear of losing his men when Samuel got delayed, performed a sacrifice unto the Lord, which was not acceptable to God and to Samuel the high priest. Invariably, this was the last straw that broke the camel's back as Samuel pronounced God's judgement upon Saul *(1 Samuel 13:1-14).*

Brother you need to pray against the demon of delay which may make anyone under pressure to do what they would not normally do e.g. due to belief that time is running out for them to achieve something so doing it the world's way or their way but neglecting God's way. E.g. Abraham accepting to sleep with Hagar in *Genesis 16:1-4.*

Making a pledge

Saul made an unreasonable vow when he was at war without telling his son. Jonathan, unaware of his father's vow ate some of the forbidden honey and he was nearly killed by his father but for the people's intervention. Father, be careful of your vows to God and people. It is better not to make any vow to God or man. Be careful not to make vows on behalf of others as well.

Run to God when in trouble

Saul did not keep in touch with Samuel and he missed out on godly counselling, provision and protection.

King Saul consulted a medium which he knew was contrary to God's law. By the time of war against the Philistines in *1 Samuel 28:1-19,* Saul became afraid and instead of turning to God, he turned to the medium. Not only was God displeased, his end and defeat was announced. Brother, who do you consult in times of the crisis or battles of life? It is ungodly to consult a medium; more so, consulting such comes with a price including exposing yourself and family to demonic operations. Many leaders instead of hiding God's words in their hearts wear ungodly bands, chains and ammunitions as if to say such things got them into their enviable positions in the first instance. Why do people listen to man's voice and not God's?

I suggest some people listen to man rather than God's voice because:

- ❖ We have the adamic nature of wanting to rebel. We sometimes think we can be wiser than our creator *(Genesis 3:4-5)*.
- ❖ God usually speaks if we care to listen but hardly puts any pressure on mankind like Satan and man do. We operate under the 'freewill' of God.
- ❖ Some people prefer to please and honour man rather than God.
- ❖ Sometimes because people are lazy to go God's way; the way of the cross is costly. Many times we are too much in a haste and impatient. We live in a fast world and for some they are actually living on the fast lane of life.
- ❖ God's instructions many times do not fit into human dreams, for example, how can baby Jesus give anyone salvation, eternal life, healing, deliverance, hope, joy, peace etc. We have always worked and earned our ways in life. Salvation is too 'free' a gift to be accepted (Romans 10:8-10). Or perhaps how could you do what the Lord is asking you with those prevailing circumstances you are in? Miracles are extraordinary actions to mankind from God. His ways are not like ours, the Bible declares.

Results of heeding to man's voice:

- ❖ Failure to accomplish God's plan for the individual. Brother, you play a significant role in your family and perhaps in the society.

- ❖ Rejection by God which eventually leads to rejection by man for only God can give a person or leader His favour (Proverbs 16:7, 1 Samuel 15:26).
- ❖ Punishment from God (Genesis 3:16-19). What a man sows that he shall reap.

Results of heeding God's voice:

- ❖ A meaningful relationship with God.
- ❖ Success in accomplishing tasks (Proverbs 3:5-6 and Joshua 1:6-8). David unlike Saul succeeded because he sought the Lord in everything he did.
- ❖ Peace within one's self and peace with others.
- ❖ God's tremendous blessings on whatever you do.

Father/brother your success is hinged on the question of whose voice you hear and obey. In you are all the resources that you need to succeed. Any tradition that seeks to put itself above God's voice must be done away with. God has chosen you but have you realised for what task, and can you honestly say you are accomplishing all that God has assigned for you to do or are successful in reaching the vast mission field in your calling? How effectively are you in disciplining yourself, family and others in the way of the Lord? Will it be God's voice or man's voice from now?

May we pray please now that you have been able to review your life in light of Saul's life.

Dear Father,

Father, thank You that I can come just as I am before You now. I have lost my job, health, marriage, child (please list them) for which I am deeply hurt, confused and angry (please feel free to express yourself). I confess I have sought for help in places and with people and things which are not of You. I have exposed myself and my family to satanic tormenting spirit e.g. by my wrong attitude, friends, company, organisations or clubs joined (please list them). I confess them as sins and against You alone have I sinned. I have been deceitful and set traps for others to kill and destroy them at home and work for reasons, which You know. Please forgive me and restore all that I have lost in Jesus' name.

Thank You Lord, for my very humble beginnings and how far You have led and blessed my life. Like Saul, I have partially obeyed You often, been impatient with You Lord to complete what You started in my life, I have tried too to help You at such times. (You may want to be more specific on these times). Father, I have since realised that this is sinful and I humbly repent Lord. You know all of the times when I have feared men instead of You Lord and have compromised in my endeavours. I ask for Your forgiveness, cleansing and restoration in Jesus' name.

I am sorry for underestimating the following people thereby hurting their feelings (you may list their names here) for reasons You know Lord. I am sorry too for seeking You less than before. Please forgive me and be merciful to me.

Father, I need Your help in finding a godly mentor in Jesus' name. Lord, please give me another chance to be who You have called and ordained me to be and with Your help and the leading of the Holy Spirit I will be all that You called me to be in Jesus' name I have prayed with thanksgiving. Amen.

Chapter 12

THE FATHER WHO FAILED TO PASS ON HIS WISDOM TO HIS CHILDREN.

Unqualified but chosen

Solomon was the second son of Bathsheba who formerly was Uriah's wife. God loved Solomon and gave him another name, Jedidiah at birth. God sent Prophet Nathan to congratulate King David on the arrival of Prince Solomon *(2 Samuel 12:24–25)*.

God's ways indeed are not like ours and often too complex for mankind to understand. Of all the sons of David, God chose to send a congratulatory message and baby's name to David after the birth of Solomon. Solomon was favoured by God above all the other children of David, while his older sibling from the same parents died from God's inflicted sickness, his own life was not only spared but blessed much more above his other siblings from the same father.

By birth and age Solomon was not qualified to become the king but God's favour and grace handpicked him. Pause, brother, and scan your life and you will see the many times God's favour had handpicked you. Brother, may you and I find favour in the sight of God irrespective of our background in Jesus' name. His parents loved Solomon. He grew up to be a poet, singer like his father. What have your children inherited from you, good or bad looks, habits or skills?

On King David's deathbed, he chose and ordained Solomon to become the next king after him *(1 Kings 1:13-40)*. His mother was very instrumental in getting him to the throne. Thank God for mothers who align their children with God's destiny for them.

Ask for divine wisdom

As soon as Solomon became the king, he asked God not for money or fame or the lives of his enemies but for God's wisdom to rule His people. God gave him this and more *(1 Kings 3:5-28)*. Wisdom, the Bible says is the principal thing. Wisdom will achieve what strength cannot achieve *(Ecclesiastes 7:11-12, 19, 8:1, 9:18, 10:10)*. King Solomon's wisdom was world known and sought after even by Queen Sheba for he ruled the people with wisdom and understanding. He was the richest King that has ever lived.

A wise person once said there is no problem but lack of wisdom. The Bible says my people perish for lack of knowledge. To be a successful person, father, husband, son, brother, uncle, nephew or leader at home or work requires wisdom. Wisdom does not come cheaply but to those who will discipline themselves and seek the face of the Lord, the giver of wisdom.

King Solomon obeyed his father by building the Lord's temple in line with all the specifications that were given to him. In building the Lord's temple and his royal palace, he liaised with many people from other countries - King Hiram of Tyre inclusive. In return for the services he received, he gave food to the King *(1 Kings 5:1-12)*. King Solomon obeyed his father, being careful to use the specified and best materials for the temple of God.

Solomon had an elaborate and befitting opening ceremony to God for the temple during its dedication *(1 Kings 8:1-66)*. Solomon gave God an unparalleled sacrifice. Nothing was too much or too big for him to give to God. To the things of God, King Solomon was very generous. How generous are you towards giving to the things that touch God and His people? How much do you appreciate where God has kept and led you so far? His unequalled gift provoked God to appear to him in the dream asking for his request.

Solomon obeyed his father in killing Joab and Shimei *(1 Kings 2:8-ff)*. Both people could have been threats to his kingdom. In wisdom, he eliminated them as soon as he got grips of the throne. Some people should not be allowed to remain in position if they are known to misuse their authority and kill others especially the innocent and the poor. They don't have to be killed physically but removed from the corridors of power so that they are no more in the position of being a threat to the poor, the innocent and the helpless.

Solomon's wisdom permeated every aspect of his life and rulership. He was much organised in his home, office, throne and vocation and for that many including kings and queen visited him to learn at his feet. They also brought for him expensive gifts. He was very much aware of nature around him including the ants, birds and animals. Brother, many will seek a wise man who they believe can help solve their problems *(Psalms 128:1-6)*. A man's gift will make room for him. There are too many problems in the world today, please ask that God will make you a solution in your area of calling.

Be organised

King Solomon was very famous for being orderly and organised. He was very famous, hardworking, and industrious. King Solomon was successfully involved in international trading including floating ships *(2 Chronicles 9:10–22)*. He ruled the people of God in peace. How orderly and organised are you brother, and do you govern your family or work in peace or with an iron hand? Is your rulership in your home, family or workplace that which blesses people or otherwise? Are you building personalities or organisations?

To be organised requires wisdom, willingness to be thorough the first time and every time after. How well brother or father are your receipts, money in your purse or pocket, clothes, shoes, books, vital documents and so on filed? Joseph and Daniel among many others were well-organised men. See *Genesis 41:46-57* and *Daniel 6:1-5*.

To be organised in the home is not solely your wife's responsibility. It could be by joint effort but you will need to take the lead in this because when you are not organised:

- ❖ you are likely not to be focussed
- ❖ you lose a lot of time looking for vital documents and relevant information
- ❖ you are more likely to miss important dates, appointments and opportunities
- ❖ you are likely to have around you a cluster of non-relevant or not so useful items that will make your life and environment untidy.
- ❖ you are more prone to being slowed down
- ❖ you are likely to experience uncalled for delays and may slow your life down
- ❖ it may drain you of the energy that could have been used for more productive things.
- ❖ it may cause unnecessary arguments, quarrels, anger, unnecessary stress and fatigue.
- ❖ If care is not taken, it might lead you to making wrong decisions if you cannot lay your hands on the facts as and when needed.

If you have to choose then please choose to be organised in every area of your life. Choose a simple method or technique, which you should consider easy for you to use and remember, easy for you to access, clear and tidy. Be organised in every area of your finance, home, career, business and relationships. Initially, getting organised can be challenging but as you are willing and disciplined you will find your life, family and environment easier to handle and less stressful.

Discover your strengths

King Solomon was an excellent judge. His unique style of judgement today is still many times better than that of the best judges even today. Some judges might even have him as their unseen mentor and ask themselves what King Solomon would have done in particular situations.

King Solomon was a poet and he wrote many songs. Among his writings in the Bible are Proverbs, Ecclesiastes and Songs of Solomon which are still very much relevant to today's living as they were when they were first written. Solomon like King David was very observant of all of God's creation, which was reflected in his writings. Observations bring discoveries. How observant are you? Solomon left a legacy behind that still speaks hundreds of years after his home-calling. Brother, what legacy are you leaving behind?

Avoid all ungodly compromise

Solomon initially loved and obeyed the Lord. However, he married many foreign women who turned his heart away from the Lord in his old age *(1 Kings 13:1-11)*. Solomon married three hundred wives and had seven hundred concubines altogether making a thousand ladies! His father's sin became iniquity in him. Solomon married many foreign women who came along with their gods and gradually won his heart to follow them to their idols, turning away from Jehovah who elected him. He even sacrificed to 'the other gods' of his wives in his old age.

Brother, the Lord who said do not be unequally yoked and talked extensively about marriage in the Bible has reasons for that. That lady might seem harmless today but will she be so tomorrow? She may appear gentle and obedient today but will she remain so when adversity or troubled times come? She may still allow you to go to church on Sundays now that you are courting or just married but will she not turn your heart away from God in your prayer time and fellowship later? Will she allow your children to be taught the ways of Jehovah?

Many men have had their destinies enhanced or terminated by their choice of marriage partners. Many who have chosen by the outward appearance have lived to regret it permanently later. Many who toyed with the idea of a wife and one or more mistresses outside or more than one wife had their lives cut short by such relationships.

Brother, please be careful who your close friends and associates and wife are. For there may come a time in your life e.g. old age or times of sickness when such people will humanly largely determine your fate. Do your close friends pray or help you through, do they lead you away from the Lord or from life?

The kingdom comprising of the twelve tribes of Israel was to be taken away from the family of Solomon because of his following other gods and his son was to be given only his tribe to rule. He started in peace with a kingdom of twelve tribes but he ended up with the Lord stirring up Hadad the Edomite and many others as adversaries to him. Sin will be punished irrespective of who commits it *(1 Kings 11:9-28).* Solomon now sought to kill Jeroboam in *1 Kings 11:40.* His action brought God's affliction on his seeds for a time to come *(1 Kings 11:39).*

Divinely train up your children

What his father David fought to get, Solomon lost and could not pass on to his children as he was in no way prepared for the throne. It may be catastrophic for someone to be promoted to a position of authority without adequate preparations. It is not uncommon for such people to misbehave and misuse the authority they have. There is an African adage that says an untrained child will sell off the family's inheritance.

It is not a sin for your children to inherit properties or wealth for that is scriptural. A good father leaves inheritance for his children's children but please take time to train, prepare and tutor your children and grandchildren to walk in the fear and obedience of the Lord and in whatever training that will be required for the wealth and position you shall bequeath to them.

Solomon's son, Rehoboam lost eleven tribes primarily due to God's previous message as seen earlier and also because he lacked wisdom in approaching the sensitive matters of the people. Rehoboam, for lack of wisdom rejected the counsel of the elders. Please note that God's anointing upon your life the father does not necessarily get passed on to your children unless they are trained, tutored for it and walk in the way of the Lord so please do not assume it will be automatically passed to them when you are no more. Now is the time to prayerfully train and nurture them in the way they should go *(Proverbs 22:6)*.

Brother, who you choose to hang out with or surround yourself with now will certainly affect you when you are old; when perhaps you would depend on them for all that you were capable of taking care of before.

Should your marriage turned out not to be as you had planned or expected, there is hope for you if you will turn it to the Lord in prayers. He is able to change your situation today if you will acknowledge your mistakes before Him and ask for His help.

God is truly a rewarder of those who diligently seek Him. May we pray please now that you have been able to review your life in light of Solomon's life

Dear Father,

Father, thank You that with Your help I have been able to study the life of Solomon and review my life. Lord, who but You could have spoken to me in the following areas (you may wish to list them).

Father, thank You for the following people who You have used to point me to my destiny (you may wish to list them). I pray Your blessings on them today and always. Help me too, to be a positive influence on others in reaching their God-assigned destiny in Jesus' name.

Father, I openly confess my past relationships with strange women (you might wish to name them and the effects of your relationships with them). Please forgive me Lord and cleanse me inwardly and outwardly for my sins. Help me Lord as I choose to walk with You from now in Jesus' name.

Father, please help me not to terminate Your blessings in my family and please show me what to do and ways to leave a good inheritance for my

children and grandchildren in Jesus' name. Help me too, to prepare them for their inheritance in You in Jesus' name.

Lord, because of the following wrong associations, I am drifting / have drifted from You to other gods such as alcoholism, pornography, occult, etc. (you may wish to list them). Please Lord, forgive me and help me to quickly from now retrace my steps back to You in Jesus' name.

Thank you Lord for the grace to read this book. Thank You Lord for the various ways You have spoken to me, met me at my points of weaknesses, struggles, aspirations and strengths. Thank You Lord for choosing me to be a father. Thank You Lord for the privilege to represent You in the lives of the members of my household and in my secular world. I realise that being a father is a challenging but rewarding task and how oh Lord I feel inadequate without Your guidance, help, presence and anointing. Father, I need You to please hold my hands in all that You have entrusted into my hands. Thank You Holy Spirit for Your divine revelations, guidance and uplifting from now on in Jesus' name I pray with thanksgiving..

There is only one Father in the true sense. He is God the Father, God the Son and God the Holy Spirit. Every earthly father was once a child. Once you decide to become a father or find yourself planned or unplanned on being a father, the best role model / mentor you can have is God the Father, God the Son and God the Holy Spirit. Spend time with Him today and see Him help you in your fatherly role to His Glory and your blessings.

Brother, I encourage you to rise up in the name of the Lord and be the father God has chosen, ordained and blessed you to be in Jesus' name. God bless you real good.

SOME INSPIRATIONAL WORDS FOR YOU:

DIFFICULT TO OBEY.

Many a times when God calls people
It could be very difficult for them to obey
Because of what the commands may entail
Because of the dangers and risks involved
Because of the timing and place of the assignment.

Imagine Abraham's call to leave his country and people
Imagine his silent grief and that of Sarah his wife
When in Egypt he told Pharaoh that Sarah was only his sister
Imagine Abraham's agony as he disposed of Hagar and her son Ishmael
Remember when he heard the instruction to sacrifice Isaac on the altar.

Joseph marrying Mary was only by God's own intervention
His trip with his pregnant wife to Bethlehem was tedious
Imagine his frustrations at their having to sleep in the stable
What's more? - Jesus' birth in such a place at such a time
The visit of the shepherds and the wise men from the east.

As if his ordeals were not over, one night later in a dream
God appeared to him instructing him to leave for Egypt
Immediately, he woke up from the dream, and he journeyed
With convalescing Mary and the new-born babe
Unprepared he left for Egypt where he was to reside for a while.

God's call on individuals demands no delay friend
Though it might be difficult to obey in the first instance
Your immediate response to His calls for that assignment
Your total dependence upon God's sovereignty and wisdom
Will see you through the known and unknown difficulties ahead.

NO CARELESS WORD.

Many words are spoken today friend.
At different places, to different people
By different authorities of different powers.

Whilst some words are carelessly spoken
Others are spoken without much thought
Others are spoken with no intention of fulfilment.

Words are carefully chosen by those in authorities
With every thought carefully weighed and translated into speech
Realising how important words are to each party.

Many leaders of old and of today friend
Have made unrealistic, unreasonable promises
Knowing full well that such cannot be kept.

Leaders or parents at some time and place
Have made promises believing they could fulfil them
Alas, they are unable as the circumstances get beyond them or their control.

Some parents have spoken to their children
Promising them what they can never afford to give
Promises that have had the children's hopes dashed.

God's words are never carelessly spoken
Whether directly to the individual, group or nation
Whether through the written words or prophetic messages.

His words will certainly come to pass friend
Irrespective of the time, place and people concerned
Irrespective of the prevailing negative circumstances around.

No careless word from the Almighty God friend
He means every word written or prophetically spoken
He watches over His words to bring them to pass.

No careless word from the Almighty all knowing God
Whether they are words of punishment or justice
Or they are words of healing, blessing or anointing.

Over and over again God confirms His words friend In the lives
of His people no matter their level of faith
At His own appointed time and chosen manner.

Friend what has God spoken to you now or before?
That seems impossible, unfulfilled or completely forgotten
It will certainly come to pass as God speaks no careless word.

Isaiah 55: 10 -11, Psalms 12:6.

© O. Ola - Ojo '91.

MEN WHO CHANGE HISTORY

Saul tarried under a pomegranate tree
And the men with him were about six hundred
But Jonathan said to his amour bearer
Let us go over unto the garrison of these uncircumcised
It may be that the Lord will work for us
For there is no restraint to Him
To save by many or by few.

Men who change history are indeed few
They are men who dare to take a leap
Holding on to their faith in God
They attempt the seemingly impossible
Men who change history do not procrastinate
Forgetting the past, they press single-mindedly forward
Never fearful, never timid and never wavering
They believe in the Almighty God and in themselves.

Men who change history neither sit on the fence
Nor play the 'blame game' on God or anyone
They are men who have a burden, a vision, and a clear mission
Men who are willing to give all even their very lives.

Numbers never move men who change history
Not the amount of the oppositions
Not the size of their own supporters
They get themselves right with God, and are in tune with Him
They are prepared to take seemingly risky steps.

Would you in the Lord's strength
Turn the tide of adversity
Like Jonathan and his aide routed the enemy's host
While Saul tarries with his host.

1Samuel 13-14:23

WHILE HE SLEPT

Many great men mightily used of God
Through whom many have been delivered
Who had led many sinners to the Lord
Being vessels through whom the Holy Spirit moves
Have been so active only when awake
How very unfortunate to see them captured
By weaklings when they were fast asleep.

Such was the case of General Sisera
Who had escaped on foot from the battle field
Unsuspecting the warmness and welcome
He entered into Jael's tent thirsty
For water he was offered fresh milk
How very unfortunate for him some hours later
'Weak Jael pegged him to death while asleep.

Samson the judge had no equal in power
Much was the anointing by the Spirit of God on him
None of his enemies could capture him when awake
Until he gave out the secret of his power to Delilah
Whilst he slept, he was disarmed and overpowered
That led to his capture, torture, and death.

Many great children of God today friend
Have been disarmed, decoded, and overpowered
They have become weaklings in the hands of the devil
They have lost the anointing of God on them
They have been ridiculed and mocked
For they have been overpowered while they slept.

Many today have slept off their responsibilities
They have gone to seek for comfortable beds
Nowhere else but in the home of the devil
They like Sisera have walked into the devil's net
Some like Samson have lusted for the devil's choice
They have been disarmed by worldly pleasures
They have lost their authority while they slept.

Controlled physical sleep is good for the body
But spiritual sleep can be very dangerous
The whole amour of God is to be worn
Permanently by the child of God
Resist the devil at all times everywhere
Remember that the world is a battlefield.

Are you asleep beloved in your Bible study?
Are you asleep in your quiet time and fellowship?
Are you asleep in your sharing with others?
Are you asleep in your God-sent assignment?
Are you asleep in the tent of Satan's emissary?
Are you asleep in the home of the unknown traitor?
Are you asleep, no more in tune with the Holy Spirit?

Unknown to you dear friend who is asleep
Satan is waiting to pounce on you as soon as you wake up
Where you thought was comfortable, neat, and nice
Where you received much generosity and welcome
Could be a death trap, covered up with nice things
Could be the very seat of the enemy of God
Be careful and alert today dear friend.

© O. Ola- Ojo. 08.04.1991

ALONE WITH GOD

Many of us want to hear from God
To listen to His small still voice
Yet we never provide such an atmosphere
And might not be quiet in our spirit
To get directives and instructions from God.

Jacob, frightened to meet Esau
On his way back home as directed by God
With two armies and many flock
Got assurance from God after wrestling with the angel
Whilst alone on the other side of River Jordan.

Great men and women in the Bible
Became great for they heard from God
Whilst they were alone with Him
They found time out of none to be with Him
In prayers and the study of His Words.

Many of us complain of our busy schedule
For some it's their children or their family or wealth
Whilst for others it's their many responsibilities
Even when alone in their closets at home
Their minds are not quietened to hear God

Alone with God my brother and sister
Get your spirit off your family and associates
Off your many duties and responsibilities
In the closet of your heart talk with God
In prayers and meditation on God's Words.

Time spent alone with God in your closet
Is time better spent than at any other time
For not only will you be reassured
Comforted, encouraged and nurtured.
It is a time of receiving clear directive from God.

Take time to be alone with God my brother and my friend
Wherever you are now and whatever you may be doing
God is ready to give you directives on your problems
For 'in returning and rest you shall be saved
In quietness and in trust shall be your strength'.

Genesis 22:9-12, 22-32 & Isaiah 30:15.
© O.Ola -Ojo 13.05.88

THE VOICE OF GOD OR MAN?

God in His mercies and love
Speaks to His children the chosen ones
Giving them instructions to obey
As well as assignments to carry out for Him.

Saul was the first King in Israel
In a battle against the Philistines
Decided and sacrificed the offerings
Without waiting for Samuel the Prophet.

Sometimes later in another war
Against the Amalekites he fought
Killing everyone he however kept
The best of the sheep, lambs and everything.

When Samuel the Prophet asked him why
On both occasions he disobeyed God
Saul's response was that he disobeyed God
Because he feared his men and heeded their demands.

Many have lost their God-given authority and positions
Of honour, authority and power
Simply because they gave heed to the voice of men
Rather than the voice of the Omnipotent God.

I'll rather obey the voice of God
Than that of any man or woman
For rebellion is as bad as witchcraft
And stubbornness is as bad as idol worshipping

The voice of God and the words of God
When given are meant to be completely obeyed
The fear of man is a dangerous trap
But to trust God means safety.

The voice of God and the words of God
When given are meant to be completely obeyed
Obedience is far better than sacrifice
And listening to Him than burnt offerings.

1 Samuel 13:1-14, 15; 1-23.
© O.Ola -Ojo 7/04/89.

OBEDIENCE IS FAR BETTER

Adam and Eve in the Garden of Eden
Were made the masters of God's creation
By disobedience, they ate the forbidden fruit
And lost their position of leadership and authority
They were banished from the Garden of Eden
Never again to enjoy the company of God's presence.

Moses and Aaron on the way to the promised land
Were God's spokesmen and prophet to the people
By disobedience, namely through annoyance
Moses struck the rock twice instead of speaking to it
They lost the opportunity of entering the promised land
And they both died in the wilderness.

Saul was Israel's first king
He went ahead and sacrificed without Samuel the prophet
He was afraid of the people of Israel
And did what they demanded regarding the loot
The Lord was sorry that He made him king
And thus rejected him as king.

Realise that God has put you there
In that leadership capacity today
Never be afraid of the people you are leading
Nor honour their ungodly demands or give in to their pressures
Seek the counsel of the prophet of God
And totally depend on God's leadership.

Obedience is far better than sacrifice
God is more interested in your listening to Him
Than in your offering the fat of the rams
Trust in God and obey Him all the way
Then will be able to lead your people to the their promised land
And receive the leader's honour.

Genesis 3:1-24, Numbers 20:1-13 & 1Samuels 16:1-30

THE DEAD END

It starts like any other useful, straight forward road
It looks so beautiful and very attractive
Very promising is the quality at the beginning
With promising signs to a destination at last.

What an unfortunate mistake to travel on it
What seemed initially attractive and beautiful
Turns out to be unending and everlasting
Turns out to be just one of the dead ends.

Every sin dear friend is a dead end
For in the end it is full of disgrace and regrets
Full of heartaches, uncertainty and hatred
Full of bitterness, pity and unaccountable loss.

No matter how small or big that sin is
No matter where, when and how it was committed
No matter whatever excuse we might want to give
It does not remove the sin from being the dead end.

Now is the time to retrace your steps friend
Now is the time to reassess the situation
Now is the time to seek the Lord's face once more
In order that you might not end up in the dead end.

The dead end has nothing to really offer you friend
It has no guarantee, no security no peace
It has no degree of commitment or improvement
It has no hope for a better future friend.

In your daily walk, dear friend
Do try and watch out for the dead end
Do not be attracted to it or trapped in it
For in the end it is going to be the dead end.

© O.Ola -Ojo 11.03.92.

OPPORTUNITY TO BECOME A CHRISTIAN

Dear Father in heaven,

Thank you for the privilege of reading this book. Indeed I have sinned and come short of Your glory. I am grateful to You for sending Jesus Christ into this world to come to die on the cross of Calvary for me. I believe in my heart that Jesus Christ paid for my sins, past, present and future. I believe Jesus Christ was buried and on the third day He rose from the dead. I believe that Jesus Christ will come back again. I confess with my mouth and I accept Him now to be my Lord.

Master, Saviour, Brother, and Friend, I ask in Your mercy for the infilling of the Holy Spirit so that with His help, I can live a victorious life becoming all that You have ordained me to be in Jesus' name. I pray with thanksgiving. Amen.

If after reading this book you said the above prayer and became born-again, Congratulations! You are Born Again is a booklet for those who have done so through reading this book. It is a free booklet that we would like you to have. In it, the frequently asked questions are answered and this will get you on the way to growing in your newfound faith in God. You can download this free booklet from our website: www.protokospublishers.com

You may also contact any of the organisations listed at the end of the book.

I look forward to hearing from you soon.
O. Ola –Ojo (2010)

Other Books By The Author:

Provocation, Prayer and Praise

(December 2004 & 2009)

Complimentary to The Christian and Infertility this book focuses on the story of an infertile woman in the Bible, her provocations, prayer and praise. Whatever makes you incomplete, unfulfilled, less than whom God made you to be, whatever issue of life that the enemy uses to provoke you calls for prayer.

Key features include:

- Some known medical reasons for infertility in the women.
- Why Hannah went to the house of God in spite of her barrenness.
- Is it true that the husband is much more than 10 sons to the infertile woman?
- When, where and how to address the source/cause of your provocation.
- God's part and your part in that promise.
- God is able to met that humanly impossible need of yours.
- A time to celebrate and praise God.

Book Details:

Paperback: 128 pages
Language English
ISBN-13: 978-0-9557898-3-0

Review:

A Reader from London, 7 Jan 2006 on Amazon.co.uk
An excellent easy to read and understand book. The principles shared in this book though primarily are for those trying for a baby could as well be applied to any area of hurt and un-fulfilment.

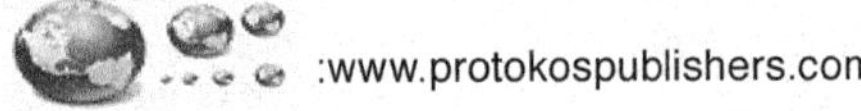

The Christian and Infertility

(December 2004 & 2009)

The Christian and Infertility addresses one of the often neglected needs of Christian couples. It gives an insight into infertility from the biblical and medical perspectives. It is written not only for potential fruitful couples but for pastors, family and friends of these couples. It is written that the Body of Christ might be fully equipped to know and support couples who are facing the challenge of infertility at present.

Key features include:

- Childleness in the Bible and lessons to learn;
- Some possible physical, medical and environmental causes of infertility;
- Some known spiritual causes of infertility;
- The man and low sperm count;
- Some of the available treatment optons in the UK;
- Choice of fertility treatment;
- Should a christian professional be involved in fertility treatment?

Book Details:

Paperback: 146 pages
Language English
ISBN-13: 978-0-9557898-2-3

Review:

A reviewer from Glen Burnie, USA, 29 Oct 2007 on Amazon.co.uk'
The book is a great eye-opener for all. It sheds light on infertility from the medical and spiritual angle. This gives the reader a balance because i believe every human being is made up of both physical and spiritual part. To get a balance in life, the two parts must be well fed. One must not concentrate on the spiritual and neglect the physical part. The book also reminds us that God has a way of sorting us out.... The book is quite inspiring. I will recommend this book to everybody trusting God for any form of blessing from God to go get one and apply it to his or her situation. It will definitely bless you and yours'.

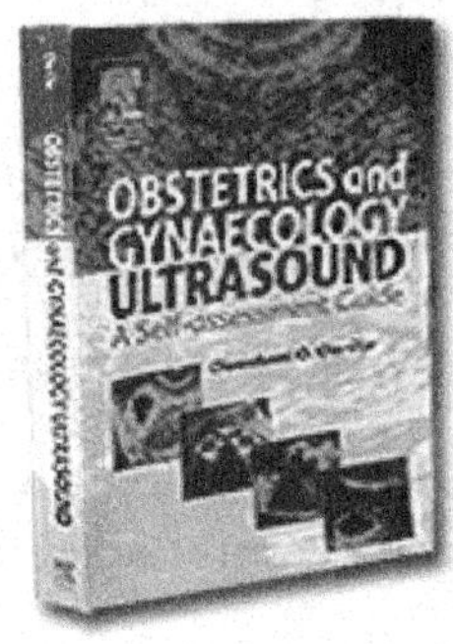

Obstetrics and Gynaecology Ultrasound -

A Self-Assessment Guide

June 2005 Churchill Elsevier Publishers, UK.

This self-assessment guide is a structured questions and answer book that develops the reader's understanding capability using a simple method in treating related topics. Clinical indications are presented with their corresponding ultrasound findings using appropriate illustrations. A case study approach is followed; presenting the clinical and ethical dilemmas that might arise whilst encouraging students to think. The aim is to reinforce theoretical knowledge within a clinical environment.

Book details:

- Over 600 high-resolution ultrasound images
- Cover a wide spectrum of ultrasound curriculum.
- Includes a detailed study of fertility.
- Aids quick understanding of subject matter.
- 468 pages.

ISBN-10: 0443064628
ISBN-13: 978-0443064623

Review:

"...This excellent new book is a study guide... This is an attractive paperback that should be essential reading for trainee obstetric and gynaecological sonographers, whether they are radiographers or radiology or obstetric trainees. It will be of particular value to those preparing for the RCOG/ RCR Diploma in Advanced Obstetric Ultrasound and to specialist registrars in obstetrics and gynaecology undertaking special skills modules in fetal medicine, gynaecological ultrasound and infertility..."

The Obstetrician & Gynaecologist, www.rcog.org.uk/togonline
Book reviews 2006

Reviewer Ann Harper MD FRCPI FRCOG.
Consultant Obstetrician and Gynaecologist
Royal Jubilee Maternity Service, Belfast., UK

:www.protokospublishers.com

GOOD MUMS, BAD MUMS

(June 2005 & 2009)

This is in two parts, the main chapter that can be used for personal or group study, and an accompanying exercise section. The privileged position of a mother is in her being a co-creator with God and bringing forth life (lives). This book compliments one of God's previous revelations to me as contained in the book titled Good Dads, Bad Dads'. While the father could be likened to the pilot of the family plane, the mother can be likened to the force behind the plane – positive or negative. Good mothers are not only co-creators with God, they also do nurture as well as nourish their children physically, emotionally and spiritually.

Keys Features:

- Were all the mothers in the Bible god mothers?
- Lessons from the strengths and weakness of seven mothers.
- Be encouraged - you are not alone in the assignment of motherhood.
- Be motivated in the areas of your strengths.
- Learn ways of supporting your husband and children.

Book Details:
Paperback: 162 pages
Language English
ISBN-13: 978-0-9557898-1-6

Review:
I appreciate the author's method of writing. It is always exciting holding her book to read. Personally, 'Good Mums, Bad Mums' has been a blessing to me in no small measure. The book is rich, it is loaded with physical and spiritual uplifting subjects. To all existing and potential mothers, this book is a MUST read. At the end of every chapter there is an exercise to do that will help in re-examining your life spiritually and in other ways. I encourage all women to get and use this book as a guide in raising their children. You will be glad you did.

Pastor Mrs T Adegoke
Freedom Arena
London, UK

 :www.protokospublishers.com

To the Bride with Love

(2007 & 2009)

Every wise woman preparing to get married knows she will need sound advice, practical tips and solid, heartfelt prayers, of those who have travelled on the road she is about to journey on. In this book, 10 women of different age groups, from different backgrounds and cultures who wedded under various circumstances, individually share their experience with the bride in an intimate, very candid and unforgettable way.

Book details:
Paperback: 108 pages
Language English
ISBN-13: 978-0-9557898-4-7

To the Bride with Love is the perfect bride's evergreen companion. The content is suitable, relevant and applicable even decades after the wedding day.

To the Bride with Love is an ideal wedding gift on its own. It can also accompany any other gift (big or small) that you have for the bride but take this hint... the bride will keep thanking you for the book years and years after.

Reviews:
'One of the best', 19 Jul 2008 on Amazon.com
Sade Olaoye "clare4good" (United Kingdom)
This book has really helped my marriage from the onset as I got it as a wedding gift, God bless the giver. It's a must read for relationship improvement and God's guidance. I recommend it for people to get it for themselves, moreover as a great blessing for someone else in love. "To the Bride with Love"

Review by **Oyinlola Odunlami** CEO.
Shallom Bookshop, London UK
The writing style of Oluwakemi is unique, peculiar and distinct to herself. I recommend To the Bride with Love to wives, wives to be, mothers, mentors, youth leaders and workers. Why? The clarity, the focus and the intent of this book is so empowering, encouraging and enlightening that it will definitely mould or re mould a life to achieve its purpose. The truth is, there are very few

books that have depth as well as help you to achieve your goals and arrive at your destination. Many books tend to excite you but have no depth; you read and you forget; they do not really change you but this book, To the Bride with Love will definitely leave a word in your spirit and move you to your next level!

I believe that this is also a book that pastors will find useful as a manual for marriage counselling, because many books on marriage focus mostly on what you as an individual can gain, your own personal satisfaction while little is said about the sacrifices involved and their importance. As my pastor usually says, it is important to learn from those who have gone ahead, understand why some were successful and others weren't, so that we won't fall where they fell, rather, we would gain more speed, achieve our goals and thereby glorify Christ.

So, I invite you not only to get a copy of this life-changing manual for yourself, but also to put it into as many hands as you can afford to, for then the world will definitely benefit and your life will be a blessing to many.

Refuge Under His Wings

"an exhaustive analysis of the Book of Ruth in the Bible. The author combines her deep Christian conviction and excellent knowledge of the Holy Scriptures to produce a must read for every Christian, married or single. The book is interspaced with beautifully written prayers, which enables the reader to pause, pray and meditate on the revelations received... The book is also loaded with poetry like 'Thy will be done oh Lord' for those who may be facing an uncertain future or on a cross road of decisions."

Dr E B Ekpo MD, FRCP
Queen Elizabeth Hospital, Christian Fellowship,
Woolwich, London. UK

"...[a] ...spiritually sound book... a fine work of thoughtful reading and study...
I therefore recommend it to every Christian, married or single....
Pat Roach Senior Pastor
New Covenant Church.
Wandsworth Branch, London. UK.

Book details:
Paperback: 100 pages
Language English
ISBN-10: 095578980X
ISBN-13: 978-0955789809

Review:
This book feeds the soul. Most of all I loved the poetry. It gives you time to savour the thoughts as reader. There is a good mix of poetry and prose.To look at the story of Ruth in depth gave good spiritual food. You can pause and take it in at your own pace.The meditation on Psalm 121 was good also. There's nothing like reading a Psalm slowly and meditating on its contents. The author's own reflections allow you to see the book through someone else's eyes. A good read.

Gaby Richards, London, UK.

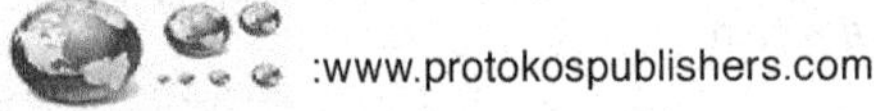
:www.protokospublishers.com

GRACE OR WORKS

This book makes you examine a lot of issues in your life, family relationships in particular, that you may have taken for granted or totally ignored. As conveyed right from the rhetorical question posed in the title, Grace or Works, the author stirs you towards asking yourself pertinent questions, thinking through for answers and even getting solutions for unresolved problems.

Have you heard of prodigal wives, husbands, mothers or prodigal fathers? This book identifies and defines them clearly. For anyone experiencing a crises in their relationship with such prodigal family members, this book, which is based on the parable of the "Prodigal son" in Luke 15:11-32 is a one-stop resource material to meet your counselling needs. And just in case you happen to be the prodigal who has caused your relatives much sorrow, there is hope for you in this book.

Interspersed with prayers for you by the author and specific prayers that you can say for yourself, as well as poems to comfort and inspire you, Grace or Works not only asks you questions, it helps you make and maintain the right choices.

Book details:
Paperback: 122 pages
Language English
ISBN-13: 978-0-9557898-5-4

:www.protokospublishers.com

THERE IS A REWARD FOR PARENTING

Man may claim that the conception of a particular child was accidental, but in God's eyes every child is in His plan and has a purpose and mission to fulfil here on earth. As a parent, teacher, church or community leader, how are you treating the children in your care?

God does not sleep nor slumber; are you sure you are doing what He expects of you as a parent or children's Sunday school teacher? What kind of reward do you expect from Him?

There is a Reward for Parenting provides a lot of answers and food for thought, using scriptural principles to show you how to ensure a good reward from God in the unique assignment of parenting and child care.

As characteristic of Oluwakemi Ola-Ojo's previous books, there is a free gift of her poems at the end of this book also, to add value to the content of the main text – making it two books for the price of one!

Book details:
Paperback: 88 pages
Language English
ISBN 978-0-9557898-6-1

Review:
The book is lovely, inspiring, very educative both spiritually and secularly.

M.F.Owoeye
Lagos- Nigeria

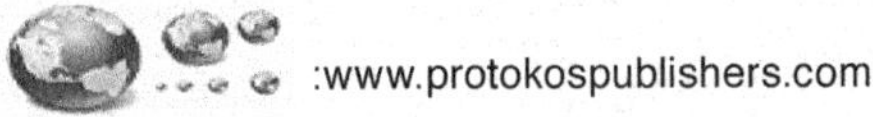

Let's Reason Together ...Youths' A-Z (Book 1)

According to the United Nations demographic statistics, the global youth population, ranging in age from 15 to 24 years, today stands at more than 1.5 billion, representing about 22 percent or a fifth of the world's 6.8 billion people inhabiting the earth. In developing nations where a greater number of this group resides, the youth population sometimes gets as high as 60% or more of the total population of such nations!

Since it is also globally accepted that the youth of any nation forms the strength of that nation, economically, militarily and/or otherwise, it is imperative that this group of people cannot be overlooked.

It is against this backdrop that the book, **LET'S REASON TOGETHER – YOUTH'S A-Z** is a timely one that is set to address the various issues that affect young people as well as their vision and aspirations. Since the primary goal of young people is to live full lives in their societies, this book examines specific elements that would help them in this process. It covers a wide range of issues from the sublime such as attitude, choices, education, health and xenophobia to the seemingly mundane such as dreams, integrity and vacation etc.

Oluwakemi Ola-Ojo has written from her wealth of experience both in the medical field as well as from a spiritual point of view and it is evident that a lot of research work was put into writing this book. Irrespective of your age and/ or religious persuasion, this book will inform and guide you.

Book details:
Paperback: 316 pages
Language English
ISBN 978-0-9557898-7-8

Reviews:
This is the most wonderful piece of youth work I have ever seen, capturing diverse situations and circumstances peculiar to youths. The work is thorough, educative and spiritually exhilarating. It is a must have for every youth worker to use, either in group discussions, seminars or straightforward teaching. This piece of work will yet raise the gospel abroad.
Dr M Akindele, Consultant Paediatrician, London, UK

This is a must read for the youths and anyone that deals with teenagers. All Sunday school staff will benefit from this book.
Deaconess B. Josiah. London, UK

Let's Reason Together ...Youths' A-Z (Book 2)

According to the United Nations demographic statistics, the global youth population, ranging in age from 15 to 24 years, today stands at more than 1.5 billion, representing about 22 percent or a fifth of the world's 6.8 billion people inhabiting the earth. In developing nations where a greater number of this group resides, the youth population sometimes gets as high as 60% or more of the total population of such nations!

Since it is also globally accepted that the youth of any nation forms the strength of that nation, economically, militarily and/or otherwise, it is imperative that this group of people cannot be overlooked.

It is against this backdrop that the book, LET'S REASON TOGETHER – YOUTH'S A-Z is a timely one that is set to address the various issues that affect young people as well as their vision and aspirations. Since the primary goal of young people is to live full lives in their societies, this book examines specific elements that would help them in this process. It covers a wide range of issues from the sublime such as anger, drugs, examination, homosexuality, jealousy and rejection to the seemingly mundane such as growth, ignorance and youth etc.

Oluwakemi Ola-Ojo has written from her wealth of experience both in the medical field as well as from a spiritual point of view and it is evident that a lot of research work was put into writing this book.

Irrespective of your age and/or religious persuasion, this book will inform and guide you. I recommend it to youths as well as parents and every person working with young people i.e. Sunday school teachers, youth leaders and pastors and social workers.

Book details:
Paperback: 322 pages
Language English
ISBN 978-0-9557898-9-2

 :www.protokospublishers.com

COMING OUT SOON

- INSPIRATIONS FOR THE MAN OF VALOUR.
- INSPIRATIONS FOR THE MAN OF COURAGE.
- MY A.B.C. OF PEOPLE AND THINGS IN THE BIBLE.

USEFUL ADDRESSES & WEBSITES

Care for the Family
PO Box 488
Cardiff
CF15 7YY
Tel: (029) 2081 0800
Fax: (029) 2081 4089
Email: mail@cff.org.uk
Website: www.care-for-the-family.org.uk OR www.cff.org.uk
Care for the Family aims to promote strong family life and to help those hurting because of family breakdown. Their heart is to come alongside people in the good times and in the tough times – bringing hope, compassion and some practical, down-to-earth help and encouragement.

Children Evangelism Ministry Inc
P.O. Box 4480
Ilorin, Kwara State,
Nigeria.
Tel: +234 31 222199
E-mail: cem@ilorin.skannet.com OR cem562000@yahoo.com
Children Evangelism Ministry Inc is a ministry that reaches out with the Gospel to children before and after birth. The ministry teaches and equips parents, teachers and coordinators of Sunday Schools and Children's Clubs. They also have and hold Children's Clubs, conferences and training seminars.

Focus on the Family
Tel: 1-800 - 232 6459
Website: www.family.org
Focus on the Family cooperates with the Holy Spirit in disseminating the Gospel of Jesus Christ to as many people as possible, and, specifically, to accomplish that objective by helping to preserve traditional values and the institution of the family.

Open Gate
2 Union Road
Croydon
CRO 2XU.
Tel: 0208 665 5533
Fax: 0208 684 7233
e-mail: opengate@yahoo.co.uk
alteschool@yahoo.co.uk
Open Gate Provides a preventative and supplementary educational facility for youths at risk of permanent exclusion. We aim at empowering and connecting the youths for the future. We provide support for the family and the community.

Protokos Publishers
P.O. Box 48424
London
SE15 2YL
www.protokospublishers.com
Protokos Publishers provides various resources for the family. We publish many life's enlightening, informative and motivational must read books. With each of our books, you are guaranteed a 24/7 counsellor by your side on the subject.

The Shepherd's Ministries
5 Brookehowse Road
Bellingham
London SE6 3TJ, UK
Tel/Fax: +44 208 698 7222
Email: info@theshepherdsministries.org
Website: www.theshepherdsministries.org
The Shepherd's Ministries helps to bring children into an experience of worshipping God in truth and in spirit; give children a world-view based on God's word and mission and helps children to exercise their gifts in local and global missions.

USEFUL ADDRESSES & WEBSITES.

Teenagers' Outreach Ministries (TOM) Inc.
Plot 85
Ladi Kwali Ext. Layout,
P.O.Box 16
Kwali, Abuja.
Nigeria.
Tel- 02082933730
Fax-02082933731
Nigeria - 08037044195, 07081860407
Email- tominthq@yahoo.co.uk
Website -www.tominternational.org
The Teenagers' Outreach Ministries (TOM) Inc. has a vision of leading today's teenager to Christ. This forms the foundation on which we mould their character in line with the word of God, thereby equipping them to fulfil their God ordained roles in life.

Total Woman Ministries
The Total Woman Ministries,
3 Herringham Road
Thames Wharf Barrier,
Charlton,
London
SE7 8NJ.
Tel: 020 8293 3730
Fax: 020 8293 3731
Email: admin@totalwomanministries.org
Website:www.totalwomanministries.org
Total Woman Ministries by God's grace has the sole vision of reaching out to women of all categories *(married, single, separated, divorced, young, middle-aged or elderly).*

United Christian Broadcasting UCB
P.O. Box 255, Stoke on Trent,
ST4 8YY, England
Among other forms of spreading the Gospel, UCB prints The Word For Today – a free daily devotional reading available for residents in the UK and Republic of Ireland

IN USA:
www.eCounseling.com
Tel Number: 1-866-268-6735

Dear Reader,

Thank you for your time and resources committed to supporting this writing ministry. Please help to tell others about how much the Lord has blessed you reading this book.

You will certainly be blessed by the other books written by Oluwakemi, so why not visit www.protokospublishers.com and place an order today.

It will equally be appreciated if you can help to write a few sentences review of the book on www.amazon.com and / or on www.protokospublishers.com.

Please note that all our books are easily available on our website and other good bookshops.

God bless you as you do.
Management
Protokos Publishers.

CPSIA information can be obtained
at www.ICGtesting.com
Printed in the USA
FSOW04n1414160916
25103FS